Hopeless in Seattle

Written by:
Daniel J. Simms

Cadmus Publishing
www.cadmuspublishing.com

NOTICE

The following book is based on true events. To protect the privacy of others, I have changed some names, dates, and times, but the content remains accurate. Furthermore, all crimes detailed herein have been intentionally modified. They are in no way reenactments of the actual crimes. Moreover, the author does not aver to the veracity of the expressions, thoughts, feelings, opinions, and emotions regarding the modified reenactments of the crimes. The sole goal of this book is to highlight the damaging effects that traumatic events like abandonment, sexual abuse, and violence have on childhood development. The integrity of this book remains intact, and nothing has been left out Thank you.

ACKNOWLEDGMENTS

There are many people I would like to thank. First, my son, Dillon. You are an inspiration son, the hardships you have been through already break my heart. I love you forever my son.

I will be the first to admit that my family is dysfunctional and fragmented. I wish that was not true. But it is. Regardless I still love them. Therefore, I would like to acknowledge my siblings David, Dennis, Douglas, and Kristine. I want them to know that despite it all I am here for them.

Due to the state of my biological family, I have come to adopt others as my defacto family. First and foremost, I want to send my love for my foster father Mike Stanton, the owner of Seattle Tree Service. He lovingly accepted and cared for me when no one else did. Thank you. I also thank Lee and Pam Stoll; you both are incredibly kind. I love you both. Thanks goes out to Don Steffins, of Edward Jones, you go above and beyond your job requirements for me, thank you for that, you are my friend. I also want to send love to my best friend Harry. I love you man.

Acknowledgement goes out to all my incarcerated family. I love you all.

Lastly, I would like to acknowledge and appreciate my various advocates. My criminal appellate attorney Corey Parker. You are a tireless defender of my rights, thank you from my heart. I recommend every inmate in need of appellate services in Washington and California to look him up. He is amazing. Next, I would like to express my heartfelt appreciation for Anne Dederer. You took on our family law case on a low-bono basis when no one else is doing anything like that for people. Let alone prisoners. Thank you. I recommend your family law services to anyone in Washington.

Dear Readers

Thank you for reading my book. I sincerely hope you become absorbed in it. When I was writing it, I imagined that I was talking to a friend or a confidant. This approach helped me immeasurably, and it also means that I consider you to be my friend. In light of our friendship, I value your comments, views, opinions, stories, and thoughts. Will you please share them with me? Please fill in your comments in the space below when you are done reading this book. Thank you.

_____
_____
_____
_____
_____

Yes, I agree that my comments, views, opinions, stories, and thoughts may be used for national publicity and advertising. I understand and agree that I will not be compensated for this authorization. By signing, you consent that your name, city, state, and occupation could be used for national publicity and advertising.

Signature: _____

Date: _____ Occupation: _____

Name: _____

Address: _____

City/State/Zip: _____

Email: _____

Phone: _____

Thank you so much for your input! Please send this to the following address:

Cadmus Publishing
Hopeless in Seattle Book
P.O. Box 2146
Port Angeles, WA 98362

FOREWORD

The goal of book one is, to encapsulate the dawn of a troubling life. It will detail fateful events, emotions, and people that shaped it. And describe the eventual true life deteriation into criminality with unmatched transparency and honesty. Supplying the reader with unparrelled access. The author captured three critical time periods. And this became the Hopeless in Seattle trilogy. It was a prudent decision. It gave us the opportunity to internalize his story and message: While providing snapshots that readers need in order to conceptionalize the detrimental effects of abandonment, abuse, and violence. The trilogy provides a never before seen glimpse at life unfolding in the worst possible way. Crime, violence, drugs, and incarceration all paved the ugly road of despair he went down. Reading the precarious journey will be heart wrenching. This is just the beginning of his odyssey. We hope you will be viscerally engaged. Becoming emotionally involved and rooting for his well-being. While wanting to save him, hold him, protect him, and console him. The story has a logical progression that flows seamlessly.

It reads as no book of nonfiction ever has. Remarkably, the last year of school that the author completed was the sixth grade. You will read why he dropped out after middle school. He was barely able to read, do math, or write, but he has managed to write this and make his voice heard.

We hope it will amaze and astound you. Please be warned some of the experiences he went through are graphic and may horrify you, surprise you, and help you truly appreciate the family and life that you have. Repeatedly, you will see how society fails to protect its most desperate members.

This is much more than a book. It is a call of action, a mobilization, and a true movement. By the end of the book, you will want to confront the broken system that repeatedly neglected him. His repeated cries for help will strike you speechless. In light of knowing what occurred to him, you will wish that you could enter the narrative to intercede on his behalf. You will want to yell at the indifferent authorities for their lack of humanity, compassion, or sympathy. To fully appreciate this story, one must intermittently stop to digest each scene. The story is so compelling and poignant that you will be physically forced to stop reading occasionally. It will be a knee-jerk reaction. If this happens to you, take that time to share your experiences online. You can use social media, such as Twitter, or you can blog or call someone. Share with them how the story has impacted you. Make this an interactive and social experience. You can help others get involved by telling them how this story made you feel. In addition, take a moment to hug a family member or anyone. You are immensely lucky to have these people in your life. Show them some love today. Have a pleasant reading experience, and thank you for joining the conversation online. We appreciate your voice.

CHAPTER 1

I sat on the front porch of my first foster home and cried for hours. The feelings rushing through me were a mixture of abandonment, unworthiness, and fear. The other emotions I felt are too numerous to list. The abandonment was so vicious and abrupt that I had not seen it coming until it was too late. There was no forewarning from my mother or my father. There was no hint that my warm, comfortable world was going to come crashing down on me. The only thing that hinted at the coming doom was the suspiciously random kindness that my mother had exhibited an hour before I was placed in the foster home. She brought me food from McDonald's and talked with me for longer than she had in years.

Both of my parents were deaf, and my father had cerebral palsy, which he ultimately succumbed to. Cerebral palsy is a defect that results from complications at childbirth. It is degenerative and incurable, and it seriously affects normal bodily movements. By the time of his death, my father was completely immobile and bedridden. Due to my parents' handicaps, my siblings and

I were fluent in American Sign Language. We were all unofficial translators for our parents. I was the second of five children. There were four boys and one girl. The girl was the youngest. The names of all four of the boys started with the letter "D." Reflecting the faith that my parents had in Christianity at the time, my older brother and I bore the names of biblical characters. From oldest to youngest, our names were David, Daniel, Dennis, Douglas, and Kristine. We were all raised in a middle-income, predominately white suburb of Seattle called Greenwood. My father worked at the post office, while my mom stayed home to care for her five kids. My parents' names were Robert and Karen.

Being raised by handicapped parents was rewarding yet challenging. The reward was diversity. I was able to experience first-hand how deaf people struggle to communicate with people who can hear. Having been given the gift of being bilingual, I am fluent in both English and sign language. Sign language is my first language. However, challenges invariably arose from my parents not being able to fully connect with us. There was a divide in communication that was hard for my parents to overcome. All of us could hear, and we suffered no handicaps whatsoever. This made it hard for them to relate to us and to ultimately raise us. It also seemed like both of my parents had problems expressing affection. This probably stemmed from their experiences in childhood, but it might have come from their handicaps. They also could not adequately express their feelings or emotions through sign language. It's very hard for deaf people to convey their emotions to people who can hear. For example, the expression "I love you" is one quick sign, but it cannot be expressed simultaneously with a hug or a kiss. When a hearing person says, "I love you," the message is delivered with a mixture of verbal and nonverbal expressions, such as a hug or a kiss. I cannot remember my parents expressing one instance of spontaneous affection. This does not mean they did not love us; I believe they did. Their love was evident, but it might have seemed to an outside observer like my parents were reserved, unmaternal, and unaffectionate. In their defense, however, I believe they expressed their love and affection in other ways. Every Christmas, for example, my parents would spend a lot of money on presents.

One year, they bought David and me matching BMX bikes. Another year, they bought David and me a big TV box that was full of GI Joe's. There had to have been fifty individually packaged figures. In addition, they enrolled David and me in a private Christian school until the fifth and third grades, respectively. Why did they only let us go to this school until then? I assume the school started to get too costly. This was a common theme throughout my childhood. I don't know whether my parents were bad at managing their money or whether having five kids caught up to them. It always seemed like we were struggling economically. For instance, the food cupboards were rarely full. I remember vividly looking for loose change in the sofa so that I could buy a cheap frozen pizza or Top Ramen noodles. We wore secondhand clothes and passed them down from the oldest to the youngest boy. My little sister Kristine got her own wardrobe, but even her clothes were secondhand. School supplies were always generic. My parents bought our shoes at a discount store. One year, I wore fake Adidas shell tops with an extra fourth stripe running down the side. I was a kid, though. Sure, I got picked on in the schoolyard, but who didn't? I wasn't mad at my parents for that. One thing they did provide was a home. As far as I could remember, we had always lived in the same one-story, three-bedroom house. I still recall the address: 9036 4th Avenue NW. When I reflect on it now, that home still brings back feelings of comfort, stability, and innocence.

Sure, my parents had their faults, but they were not violent or abusive. They might not have been able to convey their affections like hearing parents could, but I'm positive that they loved us. That's why my feelings of abandonment were even more amplified. A drug -addicted single parent on welfare didn't raise me. My parents loved me, cared for me, and sheltered me. We went to church every Sunday and Wednesday night. I was a member of Awana, a Christian version of the Boy Scouts. David and I played little league baseball. There's no disputing that I was content and happy. Looking back over more than twenty years, this was the last time I ever felt that way. Never again would I feel content or happy. I might never feel that way again. I wish this were untrue. I wish it were an elaborate embellishment to garner sympathy and sell books, but it's not. My childhood memories are so vivid, and I remember them with such fondness. They are the oases in my desert of gloom.

The day I was abandoned at the foster home started out like any other summer day. I woke up, brushed my teeth, ran a rag over my face, ate breakfast, and settled down to play Nintendo. It was the original light- and dark-gray Nintendo. I was playing *The Legend of Zelda*. This was my favorite video game then, and it still is today. The only reason it's still my favorite game today is because I haven't been able to pick a new favorite since. This doesn't mean that I would not have chosen another favorite game if my life had not unfolded the way it did. With the new technology and graphics of new gaming systems, I'm pretty sure I would have found a new favorite game. It just wasn't in my destiny to play all of the new gaming systems that came out after the original Nintendo.

As I was playing *The Legend of Zelda*, my mom told me that I would be going with her somewhere. She didn't tell me where we were going. She only told me to get ready because we were going out. This was not an odd request. My mother and father routinely requested that my older brother or I go with them on errands. As I said before, we were their unofficial translators. There were no indications that I was coming on this trip for any reason other than being my mom's translator.

As I look back now, I am in awe. How did she pack my clothes without me noticing? How did both of my parents keep their poise throughout the days, weeks, or months before they placed me in foster care? Surely, this couldn't have happened over night. It required a lot of planning. Many people were involved, so I should have had a clue that this was going to happen, but I didn't.

I had just completed the fifth grade the year before. It was the summer of 1991. I was ten years old, and I believed that I was going to start the next school year at Whitman Middle School. I was looking forward to it, since all of my friends would be going there. It was going to be a new school for me, but that didn't matter. All that mattered was that I was becoming a big boy by going to middle school. After this, I planned on going to high school and then college. From there, I'd become a pilot. I had always wanted to fly a plane. In spite of these dreams, the sixth grade would be the last year of school for me until much later.

My mom and I left the house around noon. I did not say good-bye to my big brother David, whom I idolized and looked up to, or to my younger siblings. I would have wanted to say good-bye to them, but this would have required forewarning. If my parents had thought that warning me would create an emotional scene, they would have been correct. I would have screamed, pleaded, and cried. My older brother would have stuck up for me. My younger siblings would have stuck up for me too. My parents did not want to go through that. The transition would be easier for my parents if my siblings and I did not know what was happening beforehand. For me, this was cataclysmic. Being ripped out of the only life I had ever known was more than cataclysmic; it was a life-altering catastrophe that consumed me and grew worse as further tragedies occurred.

After leaving the house, we went to McDonald's. I was able to choose whatever I wanted to eat. My antennas should have gone up then. Why was she taking me out to eat? She never did that. This was so irregular that it should have made me question her motives. We were at the McDonald's that was mere blocks from my house. If I had questioned her and understood where I was going, I could have run away from her. I would have eluded her and returned to the house. Then I could have pleaded my case to my father. My siblings could have joined in, and we could have possibly swayed my parents to let me stay. At the very least, I would have gotten to say good-bye.

Instead of questioning her motives, I gladly accepted the delightful fast food treat. If I had questioned her motives, I might have changed her mood. I did not want that, so we chatted. We signed back and forth about random stuff. We discussed nothing in particular; it was just a mutual discussion between a mother and her son. She asked me questions and I answered them eagerly and happily. It had been a long time since my mom had given me this much attention. I was lapping up the attention like it was water on a hot day. Looking back, I believe she was feeling guilty and nervous. I mistook her nervous chatter for genuine interest. I wish I wouldn't have made this mistake. But I did. I remained in my state of blissful ignorance, lovingly basking in my mother's attentive embrace.

After going to McDonald's, we drove for a while. I asked my mother where we were going. She never responded; she just remained evasive. She changed the subject to something neutral and easily forgotten. I accepted her evasiveness and sat back in my chair. I watched the streets I had always known pass by my window. Then I was getting on I-5 freeway. We took an off-ramp in the Capitol Hill neighborhood. Capitol Hill is minutes away from downtown Seattle and the Space Needle. It's also a wacky neighborhood. Within walking distance, there are many different types of people. The rich people there have mansions. The homosexual population lives around Broadway and Volunteer Park. There are also rundown neighborhoods, known as the Central District, that are infested with poverty, crime, and gangs. Therefore people from all different levels of the socio-economic ladder lived and mingled there. These different types of people make Capitol Hill a diverse community. Of course, I did not know or care about this community then. All I cared about was my community, which included Greenwood, Green Lake, and Ballard.

Finally, we pulled up to this big four-story house. There was a line of huge trees in between the sidewalk and street. I had never been to this house before. It did not look scary, but it also did not look quaint and inviting. It was just a nondescript house, and there were many more identical houses throughout the neighborhood.

My mom told me to get out of the car and go up to the porch. I obediently complied. I noticed that my mom was pulling some bags out of the trunk. It did not register these bags were full of my clothes. I thought that they were bags of Tupperware or AVON. My mom seemed to always participate in those types of things. She walked up the stairs of the porch and knocked on the door. Then she waited. Once someone opened the door, my mom dutifully set the bags down. She gave me a quick hug and peck on my forehead. While the cursory kiss lingered she faced the newcomer. Then she deliberately pointed at me while maintaining eye contact with the unknown woman. It seemed her gesture signified something important. Then she promptly proceeded to rush down the steps and into her car. She did not give me any explanation. She did, however, wave good-bye to me. Why would she do that? I desperately wanted to know was there a hidden meaning that I was oblivious to. Maybe I was being hired out to babysit, housesit, or clean. Could that be it? I did not want to face the obvious, that I was being abandoned. But my mind could not conceive any other possibility. Pitifully I seized onto the hope my mother would come back. That she only went somewhere temporarily and would eventually pick me up. Yet when I reflected on her wave goodbye I couldn't help but sense the finality of it. As though she were waving goodbye to a sailor destined to months on the high seas. It was not a goodbye of a mother temporarily leaving her son to complete menial tasks. It was a sad faced farewell from a mother resigned to sending her son alone on the rough seas of life. The realization of this was venomously denied in my ten year old mind. But even in spite of its denial, I still felt overwhelming sadness. A cold shiver went down my spine and goosebumps raised under my clothes. I was on high alert. Some monumental thing had just happened to me and subconsciously I knew that. No matter how much I denied it, internally, I perceived the danger.

On guard, I asked the woman at the door where my mom was going. She pleasantly introduced herself. Her name was Jill. She had thick curly burnette hair, a broad smile, and petite frame. Her age had to be mid to late twenties. No more than that. She carefully explained that she was a foster parent. She said that I was going to be staying with them from then on. I completely shut down. Whatever else she said was lost on me. I slunk down to the ground and started crying. I could not believe that this was happening. I was in a foster home. Why had I been chosen to come here? Had I done something bad? Were my other siblings going into foster care too? There were so many questions going through my mind, but I couldn't voice any of them. I was incapable of doing so. All I could do was cry. Jill tried to ease my pain. She tried to console me. She patted my back and calmly said things like, "It's going to be all right." She also said things like, "You'll like it here," and "Come on inside. Let me show you your new room." Her cooing only managed to drive me deeper within myself. I couldn't stop crying. The world that I had known was ending.

The porch then became my prayer sanctuaryr. I prayed fervently. I quoted scriptures that I had memorized. I asked God for help frantically. Pleading to be rescued from my abandonment. My eyes streamed with tears, and I begged to be reunited with my family. I promised to strictly obey the bible and my parents. I vowed to be a better person, a better son, and a better student.

My prayers, though, went unanswered. This was my destiny. This was my lot in life. I was to forge my own path separately from my family. One world had been closed and another world had opened. I needed to accept this as God's design, but I couldn't. My yearning to be with my family consumed me. How could I accept this? I wanted nothing more than to remain within the warm embrace of my family. My endless volley of tears expressed this desire.

CHAPTER 2

After declining Jill's invitation to come into the house, I sat on the front porch. I felt lost. I couldn't believe what was happening, and I didn't know what to do or to say. I debated running away, jumping on a bus, and finding my way back home like a puppy, but I did not have any money for bus fare. I had no clue how to find my way back home, and I could not disobey an adult. I was not a troublemaker. Instead of causing trouble, I cried for hours. Nobody cared, though. Physically and emotionally, I was alone on that porch. I was alone in the world from then on.

Through my tears, I looked in horror at the objects on the porch: long chainsaw blades, chainsaws, and sharp and pointy metal spurs. Why would Jill have these things? My mind was racing. I still could not move. I was a good kid. They could use these chainsaws to chop me up. These thoughts added to my misery.

After a few hours, a big semitruck pulled up to the curb. There was a yellow machine hooked up to it. A guy jumped out of the cab and ran up the stairs. I was still huddled on the porch. He knelt down kindly to me and introduced himself. His name was Mike. He had sawdust all over himself. I realized that he was an arborist. These were his chainsaws and spurs. He had dark black hair cropped close to his scalp. A natural swoop pushed his bangs upward in a cowlick. His skin was deeply tanned from the many workdays in the sun. Like Jill, he was in his mid to late twenties. When he smiled his whole face radiated kindness and genuine compassion. He did not look dangerous at all. For that matter, Jill did not look dangerous either. This did not reassure me, though. I still felt scared, alone, and abandoned. I had been abandoned like a piece of garbage. It would have been better if I had been abandoned at a church or a firehouse as an infant. At least I wouldn't have known any different. I would have been raised as an adopted infant and set on a path of law-abiding success. Maybe I would have become a pilot. Out of five siblings, I was the only one my parents had placed into foster care. The rest of my siblings remained with my parents.

Finally, I had to face my fear and enter the foster home. Jill introduced me to the other foster kids. Three girls and two boys. When counting myself, the gender balance was perfectly matched. The oldest of the girls was Loretta. She had an open affable personality. Always eager and happy to talk, or include people in whatever she was doing. She had brown hair, blue eyes, and an adventureous personality. She was fun to be around. Jessica, Holly, and Justin were all siblings. The oldest, Jessica, had long stringing blonde hair, blue eyes, and a reserved desposition. Holly and Justin also had blonde hair. Holly wore hers in a bob fashion. While Justin had a close cropped buzz cut leaving only an inch of hair on his head. Patrick was a character. His sole pleasure in life was to talk. He loved it. From asking questions to elaborate stories. Matter of fact, he talked so much that he became a nuisance. He literally talked your ear off. It could get quite annoying to say the least. His dark brown hair was also in a close cropped buzz cut. There was another thing that stood out about Patrick, his fashion sense. He didn't have any. But in his defense, who did at nine years old. He wore suspenders with everything. And he was sure to keep his pants pulled up far enough so you could see his striped tube socks. But underneath his geeky exterior was a good natured little boy. Loretta was twelve. Jessica was eleven. Holly, ten. Justin, eight. And Patrick was, of course, nine years old. One thing that all of them had in common was a particular look. At first, I couldn't put a finger on what it was. I was puzzled by it. It wasn't until I caught Jessica sitting alone that I finally realized what it was. And once it dawned on me, I wondered if I had the same look. I knew it was possible. It was a look of forlornness. An unspoken deep sadness emanated from our souls it's like something inside of us was crushed and stepped on. And what's remarkable is I've seen the same look on many other kids since. Mostly foster kids. It's etched into their skin. Their eyes. And even their personalities. It seems to be an ageless sad maturity. A maturity that tells the world that I've been through a lot. I've been hurt. Abused. And abandoned. For the most part, we had. Mike and Jill also had a newborn son named Charlie. Knowing that there were other kids like me in the home did little to alleviate my sadness. I still felt abandoned, unwanted, and afraid. However, I eventually suppressed these emotions. Eventually, I was able to accept and deal with my predicament.

As the days went on, I found Mike and Jill to be very kind. They accepted me without question. They tried to help me overcome the tragedy that had befallen me. This was not an easy feat. On some days I could cope and open up. On other days, though, I would remain uncommunicative, rebellious, and emotional. It seemed like even time, compassion, and acceptance failed to heal my emotional wounds.

Through the remaining days of that summer, I slowly became friends with the other foster kids. We had free reign over an enclosed yard on the side of the house. We would play baseball and soccer. Video games were not allowed, but we still found ways to occupy our time.

Eventually, I was allowed to call my siblings. The calls just managed to aggravate my raw emotions. Until many years later, my parents did not disclose their reasoning for abandoning me. Their reasoning mattered little, though; the damage had already been done. No amount of crying, pleading, or begging would reverse their decision. My spirited attitude and my outgoing personality had been crushed, and I would never repair these aspects of myself.

When the school year started, I was enrolled at Meany Middle School, which was a predominately African American inner-city school. I knew no one, and I made no friends. Bullies constantly picked on me. My grades started slumping. I was miserable. There must have been a target on my back. Getting bullied was an everyday occurrence. I tried to fight back; but I was always unsuccessful. There was little that anyone could do for me, but I did not give anyone the chance to help me out. I suppressed everything. I was unwilling to share my troubles with anyone.

As the days turned into months, Mike tried to help me open up and forget my troubles. He seemed to sense my inner turmoil. We would go to the movies and talk directly to each other. He introduced me to hiking, camping, and eventually hunting. We took classes on firearm safety together. This helped me become comfortable with firearms. We would practice shooting regularly. Ironically, my comfort with firearms would eventually save and harm me simultaneously. Mike seemed to genuinely care for me and the other foster kids. On more than one occasion, he took us to the amusement park. Despite his tact, I remained shy, meek, and withdrawn. On my birthday, he bought me a Mongoose BMX bike. Out of the blue, he also gave me a boa constrictor. We spent hours putting together from scratch a big see-through enclosure for it. But the gifts and the attention that Mike gave me were wasted. How could I feel worthy of them? I was worthless.

I felt like garbage.

I was allowed to go home and visit my family occasionally. Each visit was painful. I wanted to come back home. I had been in the foster home for a year, and nothing was going to change. All of Mike's attempts at facilitating a smooth visitation failed miserably. The visits were a struggle for everyone. I would cry and plead. I would hold onto my mom or run and hide. I did not want to go back to the foster home. Mike would be forced to peel me off of my mom or run and find me. I was inconsolable. How do you tell an eleven-year-old boy that his parents don't want him? How do you tell him that no matter what he does or says, he is still not welcome at his home?

Every time I visited home, I would work tirelessly around the house. I'd clean dishes. I would vacuum and wash the cars. I would eagerly interpret things into sign language for them. I would mow the yard. I would do anything to please my parents, but my efforts were as futile as Mike's efforts. Nothing seemed to change their minds. They refused to budge. Repeatedly, my eleven-year-old mind would ask, "Why will they not take me back?"

I finally found some pleasure in starting my own landscaping service. Mike encouraged my entrepreneurship. I loved pushing the lawn mower across the neighborhood. I loved finding customers, putting up signs, and passing out fliers. I even made some business cards. With the profits, I bought landscaping tools. First, I bought an aerator. Then I bought an edger and a Weedwacker. I was a one-man operation, and I was getting used to being alone and not depending on anyone. Maybe this wasn't normal behavior, but it was my life. I learned quickly that I couldn't escape the reality of being truly alone in the world.

As my enterprises expanded, my customer base also expanded. I found myself working every day after school. I also worked on holidays and weekends, and I loved it. The work gave me a reprieve from my unhappiness. It provided an outlet for me to unleash my frustrations. Every day was a different challenge. I had to manage my work efficiently, deal with marketing and advertising, field business calls, and provide estimates. My confidence and pride expanded along with the business. Then fate intervened and shattered it all. My business, my confidence, and my pride popped like a bubble.

It was a bright and sunny day when it happened. I was pushing my lawn mower and tools around the neighborhood and soliciting work. If I had a customer at one home, I would routinely solicit work from their neighbors. This was an efficient way to not waste time and energy. On this particular day, it was hard to find new clients, but this never deterred me. I would always continue soliciting until I found a new client or it was time to call it a night. One day, I knocked on the door of a big house, and a Jesuit priest opened the door. I started giving him my business introduction. I knew he was a Jesuit priest, because, my various landscaping jobs put me around many different types of people. And on occasion I'd work for Catholic customers. The diversity of Capitol Hill included many Catholic institutions. There was two separate private Catholic schools. One for boys, and one for girls. Two Catholic churches. And a Jesuit ran University. Seattle University. It was fairly easy to discern a Catholic priest from a Jesuit priest.

Although the Jesuit Order is a subset of the Catholic Church, they are fairly independent and autonomous from them. The Jesuit Order is widely known for their vow of poverty. To live amongst the people without excess or riches. Which, I might add, is very humble and for the most part noble. The priest had a gleam in his eye. I could detect that he was interested. I was correct in thinking that he was enthusiastic about hiring me for some type of landscaping job. He said that he had some landscaping tasks that I could do for him. I followed him to a side yard. Refusing to be specific, he vaguely described the tasks that I would need to do. It seemed like he was procrastinating, wasting time, and waiting for some unseen moment. Why was he doing this? As a child, I was ignorant of any ulterior motives. I followed him innocently, and we reached a somewhat secluded area against the wall of the house. The side yard had overgrown bushes and hedges surrounded us, and the street was not visible. Suddenly, the priest was blocking the entryway. His movements still did not alarm me. After all, this man was a priest. He was a man of God. When he invaded my personal space, though, I started to feel like he was uncomfortably close. I finally sensed that something was wrong. I began to notice his big physical presence for the first time. Alarm bells started ringing loudly in my head. I attempted to calmly leave the enclosure, but this did not work. He anticipated my moves. I fell right into his grasp. With one hand, he firmly held me and blocked me from escaping. His other hand went down my pants, and he fondled me. I was in extreme shock, and I temporarily froze with fear. I was mortified. I pleaded with the priest to stop, but I could not dissuade him. His eyes were emitting lust, and his mouth was spewing promises of money and pleasure. His hands were hungrily holding and fondling me. Feeling powerless and incapable of fending off his advances, I cried. My crying turned into wailing. The wailing turned into screaming. My screaming finally broke his advances. This gave me the courage and the leverage to struggle and scream louder. I finally had the upper hand. I loudly wiggled past him and ran to the street. I almost left my lawn mower and my tools behind, but I ran back, grabbed them, and then quickly ran home.

The fear did not dissipate. I ran until I could not run anymore. Thankfully, the priest did not give chase. Breathing hard and exhausted, I started vomiting. I threw up everything that I had eaten that day. I struggled to push the lawn mower and carry my tools. Luckily the only tools I brought with me were an aerator, small hand shears and gloves. I could have had more. That day I left the bulky edger, Weed wacker, and hedge trimmer at the fosterhome. I kept the light weight tools inside the grass catcher.

That way I could push my mower without lugging tools around. I was miles away from my foster home, but I did not stop. Wanting nothing more than to lie in my bed, I hurried back. I had gained my composure by the time I arrived. Embarrassed and ashamed that this had happened, I did not tell anyone. I tried to suppress it. I tried to forget that it had even happened, but this did not work. I could no longer carry on this business. Every time I thought about working, I would feel frightened about the prospect of this happening again. I would carefully observe all strangers and watch their movements, their expressions, and their demeanors. I no longer saw prospective customers. I just saw prospective abusers. My customer base slowly withered away. My advertisements fell down, deteriorated, and blew away. I never replaced them. My business cards went unused.

My days once again fell into endless nothingness, and I did not attempt to find any activities to fill them. I fell back into a deep depression. A cloud of despair followed me everywhere. My head remained downcast. My demeanor indicated my constant state of misery. I rarely talked to anyone. Every verbal exchange was a test of patience for anyone who tried to engage me.

As before, I found solace in my infrequent visits home. When I saw my siblings and parents, I immediately came out of my depressive state. Words could not explain what it felt like to reconnect with them. It was like the darkness had been lifted. It felt like the sun was coming out after days of gloom and rainy weather. It was amazing. Then it would end, and I would be forced back into the exile of the foster home.

One evening, I received some news from my brother David. Our parents were getting divorced. My father's cerebral palsy was deteriorating badly, but he was not fighting it. He did not fight for custody of any of my siblings either. He just returned quietly to the home of his parents in Tennessee. My mother was left with the house and the kids. She quit going to church. She quit socializing with her Christian friends. She found new friends who drank and smoked. Soon thereafter, my mother began to drink and smoke.

When I visited after my parents got divorced, the environment was completely different. The orderly, clean home of my childhood was gone. It was now full of dysfunction and neglect. My mother no longer kept up any pretenses. She did not care that the house was a mess. The cupboards were empty and the kids were starving, drinking to excess was all that seemed to matter to my mother. Her parenting skills were entirely depleted, and she allowed David to have free reign over the home. David invited his friends over. Why wouldn't he do this? He was a teenager. Our mother bought beer for him and his friends. More people started showing up and staying longer. People were fornicating on the floor. Gang members would show up flagging colors. Mostly blue. They'd wear blue Dickies, work pants, Ben Davis button-ups, blue All-star converse shoes with fat blue laces, and they always had a blue bandana hanging out of their back left pockets. They were Crips. And they were proud to bang it. Letting the world know of their gang status. They began showing up to party. Occassionally they'd conduct drug deals there. But the main reason was to drink, fight, and mess with girls. There wasn't any type of authoritative presence, therefore, they got away with whatever they liked. Who could stop them? The environment was loose and unrestricted.

In this changing environment, I took advantage of the chance to be reunited with my siblings and my mother. I started fiercely lobbying my mother to let me come back. When I would show up for visits, I would refuse to go back to my foster home. I would run and hide for hours. I would wait until I knew for sure that Mike was gone. I would then sneak back into the house and sleep. My mother would see me, but she neither encouraged nor discouraged my efforts. Mike would show up daily. Sometimes he would show up multiple times in one day. Having seen the deteriorated environment, he knew that this was no place for me. I evaded him, though, by remaining especially vigilant and watching for any signs of him. Finally, he came over to the house when I was not expecting him. As he knocked at the door, I crawled out the back window. In my twelve-year-old mind, he was the enemy. He felt like part of a system that was bent on separating me from my family. I did not understand the implications of my staying in this new environment. Mike understood this, though. He knew that it was severely detrimental for me to stay in that home. He tried vigorously to take me back to his house. After I crawled out the back window, someone saw me and told Mike where I was. He ran relentlessly around to the back and then caught a glimpse of me running away. It didn't take long for him to catch up. I was a hundred feet away from him, and I kept running. Finally, he yelled, "Daniel, I just want to talk to you. You don't have to come back to the foster home unless you want to. Please stop." Even though I desperately wanted to stay with my family, I stopped running. I knew that he cared for me. He wouldn't hurt me or force me to do anything that I didn't want to do.

He voiced his fears. He said that I should come back to the foster home. He said that he was worried that the environment at mother's home would corrupt me. I had made up my mind, though. I wanted to stay. His protesting failed to persuade me to go with him. At the end of this emotional confrontation, we both knew that things would be forever different. Reluctantly, he gave me some insightful advice. He said, "Daniel, if you stay here in this environment, you will either end up dead or in prison." I venomously denied this prophecy, rebutting it with meaningless banter, but I never forgot what he said. I never forgot the look of dread on his face. He said this with certainty and conviction, and he was right. He was more right than I ever could have known at the time.

Mike never came back around looking for me after that. He accepted the horrible decision that I had made. He returned to his foster home and family, leaving me behind. To this day, I do not blame him for this decision. I had made my choice. My mother's home continued its downward march into anarchy and neglect. The neighbors had once been friendly, but they became hostile. They disapproved of the loud, obnoxious teenagers who were always binging on alcohol. They began calling the police. People would run and jump out of windows to avoid the police. It was unimaginably volatile. One minute it would be peaceful, and the next minute it would be violent. Drunken bloody fighting matches occurred daily. I was scared, but I was with my family. Regardless of the deteriorating environment, I planned on staying. This was my home, and I was extremely happy to be back.

David and I were enrolled in school. He went to Ballard High School, and I finally was going to Whitman Middle School. No longer the disciplinarian, my mother tacitly allowed us to sleep in and miss school on numerous occasions. Tragically, she neither approved nor disapproved of what we did. If she had assertively commanded control of us, we would have complied. None of us were particularly happy with this reckless living arrangement. We were kids. We wanted guidance, but we only got silence.

Then one day, things started to happen. My mother contacted her mother. My grandmother arrived at the house soon thereafter. She began packing some of our clothes. I knew what this meant. I ran out of the house and stayed at a friend's house until nightfall. When I returned, my three younger siblings were gone. My mother had turned them over to my grandmother. I remember wondering if I should have gone with them. Maybe things would have turned out differently. But it was too late. I had missed my second chance at achieving some semblance of normalcy. I would not get a third opportunity.

It might have seemed impossible, but after my younger siblings left, the situation at the house got worse. Gangs, unruly teens, and misfits took over. People began staking out territories in the house, claiming domain over rooms and makeshift enclosures.

The strong ones pushed the others around, beating them out for the prime real estate. Needless to say, I lost my room in one such battle. A big black guy named TK took it over. Shucking and jiving, he tried to verbally talk me out of it. He talked really quickly about how he needed my room. I rebuffed his slick talk, but my attempts were useless. He had other methods of getting what he wanted. Before I knew what had hit me, I was on the ground. The blow to the chin had knocked me out instantly. When I came to, he was bent over me. He whispered, "This is my room now, white boy." How could I defend myself? He was huge, or at least he seemed huge to me at the time. He was at least twenty years old, and I knew that he had been to prison before. I accepted my defeat, bowing my head meekly and leaving my room.

From then on, I felt like an alien in my own home. I tried to adapt to the lawlessness. I tried to appear tough, but it was no use. I wanted things to return to how they had been before the divorce. I wanted to feel the security and safety of a family unit. This was hell. No matter how much I disliked it, though, I still wanted to stay. I had made my choice. I planned to stay with what remained of my family: my mom and my brother David. We were still together. I loved them, and I would never abandon them. Unfortunately, they did not feel the same way about me.

CHAPTER 3

T he day started out like any other. I woke up and stepped between drunk and drugged-out bodies. I went to the bathroom, brushed my teeth, combed my hair, and rummaged through the cupboards for a morsel of food. We rarely had any food. Occasionally, someone would go to the food bank or use food stamps, but on this day there was nothing to be found. I went scrounging among the lifeless bodies, looking for scraps of fast food that someone might have left behind. I found some stale fries and a couple of partially eaten hamburgers. It was substance—something to get me by until I could find something else.

I caught my mom's eye as I was eating the scraps. She gave me a smile. I smiled back. Her smile, however, was not reflected in her eyes, which belied an undercurrent of unknown intensity. I asked her if anything was wrong. I asked if I could do anything for her. The house was in shambles, but I went out of my way to be helpful and subservient to my mother's needs. She denied that anything was wrong, nonchalantly shrugging off my inquiries.

Although I went along with her, I noticed something suspicious about her facial expression.

It seemed as though my mother was transforming along with the environment. The worse the environment got, the more she changed, until she had morphed into a mere shadow of herself. She no longer had an air of self-confidence. Instead, she projected uncertainty, aloofness, and indecisiveness. It was like she was questioning every move she made. Maybe she regretted this new environment or her decisions to backslide so far into sin. I like to think that this is how she felt. This new life of lowered inhibitions did not fit her. I still looked upon her with love and respect, but her compassionate motherly image had vanished. The weeks and months of partying had lowered her matriarchal status immeasurably. I believe that she knew this. She knew that she was failing her kids. The booze probably dulled her sense of failure, but it could not erase it. I still harbored hopes that my mom would halt her downward spiral. I hoped that she would embrace her duties as a mother.

I wanted her to banish the vices and the people that were destroying our family. But she did not do this, and she would not do this for many years. This was just the beginning of her downward spiral.

A while later, my mother requested that I go with her somewhere. Ever the subservient son, I went with her willingly. I was yearning for my mother to fully accept me, and I was willing to do whatever it would take for my mom to love me as much as possible. I did not want to be abandoned again, and she knew this. On the rare occasion that I rebelled or tested my boundaries, she would threaten to place me back into the foster home system. I could not let that happen, so I rarely rebelled or tested my limits. I would do whatever she wanted me to do. I was positive that if I followed her directives, regardless of whether or not she was sober, she would let me stay with her. But I was wrong—very wrong.

We drove to a clothing shop called Chubby & Tubby. It was a small store that offered a variety of fashionable clothes. My mom picked up some items. Then she told me to pick out an outfit and a pair of shoes. I wasn't expecting her to say this. Questioning her motives, I looked into her eyes. I did not want to get blindsided again. She occasionally would do nice things like that. Ever since the divorce, she had money. Since these acts were infrequent and subject to her whims, I remained skeptical. I warily picked out an outfit and a pair of low-top Converse All-Stars. We rung them up and stepped out. I should have been happy, but I could not shake my apprehensiveness. I remained in a state of quiet cautiousness.

I immediately began questioning her once we were heading in the opposite direction of the house. She tried to bat the questions away with ambiguous statements, such as "Wait" and "You'll see." She would also say, "It's a surprise," and "You'll like it." The blood instantly drained out of my face. I was flushed with sadness and despair. It wasn't any surprise. I was not going to like where I was going. My mother was abandoning me again. I was going to be alone again. The revelation shook me. I felt it deep in my bones. I tried to plead with her, vigorously defending why I should be allowed to stay with her. Her sense of uncertainty, aloofness, and indecisiveness was gone. She was as unwavering as a rock. There were no doubts in her facial expression or body language. She was certain. Once again, she was confident in her decision to abandon me.

We drove past my old foster home. Then we drove past Capitol Hill, downtown Seattle, South Seattle, Federal Way, and SeaTac. An hour or more away from our home, we took an exit to Auburn. She probably did not want me to live any closer to her than this. She knew that I would try to come back home, and she couldn't let that happen. She wouldn't want me popping back up on her doorstep. She found the foster home that was the farthest away. I did not get to say good-bye to my brother or to any of my friends. I should have been used to this type of treatment. I should have been able to shrug this abandonment off like it was no big deal, but I couldn't do this. It felt even worse then than it had the first time. This time there were only three of us in the family. I thought that we were tighter. I thought that we would stick together no matter what happened, but I was tragically wrong.

We pulled up to a big building that looked like a barn. Someone had refurbished it into a group home. It was situated next to the Green River and surrounded by green foliage. There was a gravel driveway, and the paint job on the house had been done recently. It was white and it had blue trim. There were a few cars parked around the building because the staff had to have cars. There was no other way to get there. The group home was miles away from the nearest city. No buses came out here. If you did not have a car, you would have to walk for hours.

My mother jumped out of the car, walked up to the door, and knocked. She tried to signal me to follow her, but I refused to go in there. I stubbornly planted myself in my seat. A man and a woman answered the door. Since I wasn't there to interpret for my mom, they all went inside. They were probably finding a pen and some paper so that they could communicate. After ten minutes, my mom came back out with two men. Unlike Mike and Jill, they did not appear to be kind. One was tall and the other was short and chubby.

They did not introduce themselves or cajole me in anyway. They were curt and matter-of-fact. They notified me that I was being placed in their care. I spoke through my tears and told them that I refused to go with them. It was like they already knew this. To them, my refusal was a foregone conclusion. They were merely waiting for me to be uncooperative. They acted like this was a frequent response. Looking at each other, they exchanged some unspoken message. The tall man walked over to open the door on the driver's side and leaned in. He looked gleeful about using force. I dug into the seat and held on with all of my might. The tall guy started pushing me out of the passenger door. The chubby guy started pulling me with reckless abandon.

Remaining rough and firm, I cried and tried to hold on, but it was no use. They were too strong, and I was too weak. I wrestled with them as they drug me into the house. I held onto every doorframe and anything I could grab, but it was useless. These were two grown adults. I should have complied, but I didn't. I struggled and fought them as much as I could. The whole time, I maintained eye contact with my mother and pleaded with my eyes full of agony. I would have done anything to stay with her and David.

In retrospect, her lack of maternal instincts was incredible. Mothers are biologically designed to protect their children. From the moment of childbirth, this primal instinct is deeply rooted in the psyches of new parents. Parents should be willing to sacrifice their own lives in the defense of their progeny, but this was not the case in my situation. My mother watched dispassionately as these men roughly manhandled me, dragging me through the gravel as I clawed frantically at the ground to find something to brace myself with. As I struggled, blood and bruises began to appear. I'd like to think this tore her up inside. I'd like to think that my intense battle to stay with her made her regret her decision, but I cannot believe this. I was not legally required to go there. I had broken no laws. Child Protective Services had not ordered me to be removed from my home. My mother was the sole proponent of this course of action. This revelation was painful for me to acknowledge, but I denied it for years. I would pretend that an unseen entity was behind my abandonment, but the truth remained hidden for a long time. Only recently have I been able to grasp this tragedy. Its impact did not soften with age. As an adult, I feel profoundly hurt that my mother could have stopped that process then. With the privilege of hindsight, I am able to reflect on this traumatic experience and the impact that it had on me. I understand the cause and the effect—the alpha and the omega. This is what made me the person I am today, and it has left me breathless. I understand everything completely, and I am haunted by my knowledge of what happened after I entered the group home. Without a doubt, I am the product of my experiences.

The two men forced me into the group home. They dragged me down the hallway, pulled me up some stairs, threw me into a bedroom, and shut the door behind them. I was incredibly exhausted by the vicious struggle. Unable to do anything but cry, I lay on the floor. Incapable of digesting my surroundings, I passed out. I found peace in my dreams, but then I woke up to the nightmare of being in an unfamiliar place. It was a nightmare that I could not wake up from. I was in a room with two beds. One bed had folded linens on it; the other bed had been tightly and flawlessly made. There was one window between the beds. Outside, nightfall had arrived. Someone had turned on a lamp for me to see by. I had wounds on my hands, elbows, and knees. I had cuts, splinters, rug burns, and bruises. My skin was covered in dried blood. My new shirt was stretched and ripped. My new pants were dirty and rubbed down at the knees. The shoes were still new, but they needed to be cleaned of the grime and dirt that had collected on them. The day's events were visible on me.

My mother's logic was remarkable. She took me to McDonald's and gave me attention on my first trip to the foster home. On this trip, she bought me a new outfit and some shoes. These small deeds must have assuaged her guilt. These deeds were not for my benefit, and I could not care less about them. They in some way provided her a measure of relief from the pain that I hope she felt. I cannot discern a different motive. Logically, she must have comprehended that they were inconsequential deeds in comparison to the anguish she had inflicted on me. Material things, though, could never extinguish my anguish. Maybe she believed that I would forgive her if she did something nice. I can only guess what her reasoning was.

After taking in my new environment, I gathered my wits to brave whatever was beyond the room. I needed to clean my wounds, use the bathroom, and throw water on my face. Slowly, I pulled the door open and peeked out. My eyes and demeanor betrayed my emotions. I was scared. An adult had never treated me so roughly. I did not want to be treated that way ever again. Slowly, I crept out into the hallway and nervously looked for the bathroom. Finally, I found it a couple rooms down from mine. The bathroom was empty of any personal hygiene products. There was no sign of a toothbrush, toothpaste, shampoo, or a comb. I found a bar of soap and a towel, but that was it. The bathtub was empty too. I hurriedly washed my wounds off, threw water on my face, and dried off. These motions offered me reprieve from my thoughts, but not much.

I knew that I had to confront my new plane of existence. There was no easy way to do so. The situation was particularly hard to deal with because I knew that my mother had brought me here against my will. She had not carefully coaxed and cajoled me into this. I just cleaned the wounds that physically displayed my struggle. I was incredibly heartbroken. Like a puppy that was scared of getting beaten, I slunk down the hallway. Attracted to the light, I ended up in a room that had been turned into a makeshift office. I entered it. A lady was in there, and her back was facing me. I said, "Excuse me, and miss. Can you tell me where I am?"

She turned in her chair with a stern expression on her face and said, "Yes I can, but first you need to step out of the office. Residents are not allowed in here."

"I'm sorry," I said, stepping out into the hallway.

"You are at Auburn Group Home," she responded.

"Do I have to stay here?" I asked innocently.

Laughing cruelly, she said, "This is your home. Nobody else wants you." I remember that her statement carried such a shocking degree of finality. Inside, I felt like she was right; no one wanted me. She had revealed my situation with such blunt honesty. I denied her accusation, though.

"Yes," I said. "Someone does want me. You don't know what you're talking about." Fresh tears welled up in my eyes.

"If you say so. Are you hungry?" she asked.

"Yes," I said, trying to stifle my tears.

She took me downstairs. In the living room, I saw around eight or ten kids and adults. The kid's ages ranged from eleven to seventeen. There were not any girls. The woman who worked there took me to the living room and introduced me to everyone. No one seemed especially cheerful. It was a somber introduction. They looked like they knew that the days ahead would be miserable for me. They offered me silent downcast warnings for the future.

The same stern dark- haired wrinkled old lady that brought me downstairs prepared a dish of food for me. It was left overs. And it reminded me of hospital food. There were no spices in it to flavor it up. But, nevertheless, I ate it without preamble, deriving no pleasure or comfort from it. It was just something to fill my empty stomach. When I was almost finished with my meal, a kid who was about twelve or thirteen came up to me.

"Hi! My name is Mike," he said. His face was sincere and he smiled broadly.

"I'm Daniel," I responded. I tried to return his smile, but I was not quite able to.

"I heard you come in earlier today. You're my roommate," he told me.

"That's cool. What's this place like?" I asked him curiously.

Giving me a serious look, he said, "It sucks!"

I told him that his description expressed my opinion of the place so far. He showed me around after that. He introduced me formally to a couple of different kids. He pointed out the exercise room and the bathrooms. We walked up the stairs to our room, and he told me that our beds had to be made the way that his was. I did not know how to make my bed so tight and flawless. So, he showed me. He told me that there were all kinds of rules and chores I'd have to remember. The staff members would inspect our room every morning. We would need to vacuum, wipe down, and dust the room. We would need to make our beds and clean the windows. They strictly enforced this daily regimen, and they swiftly applied punishments. In addition to cleaning our bedroom daily, they assigned us other chores. These chores varied. For my first week, I had to wash the dishes. For my second week, I had to take out the garbage. For my third week, I had to vacuum the hallways and the rooms downstairs. If the staff members deemed you insolent or you broke a rule, they might assign you more grueling work, such as mowing the lawn, weeding, raking, shoveling snow, picking up litter, cleaning the cars of the staff members, cleaning gutters, or cleaning the outside windows. The tasks and chores were not burdensome, but the manner in which the staff members assigned the tasks and chores was demanding. There were time constraints. There were attitude checks, arbitrary inspections, and vague demands. If you did not complete your task or chore within a particular time frame, you would be penalized. While you were completing a given task or chore, your attitude had to be jovial, upbeat, and positive. Otherwise, they would penalize you. They inspected each task or chore zealously and arbitrarily. For example, if you missed one leaf, they would deem your whole task invalid and assign you another grueling task or chore. This could go on indefinitely. Staff members could demand that you complete a given task or chore in some unknown or vague way. For instance, they could order you to mow the yard with sheers, rake the leaves with your hands, or clean the cars of the staff members with a toothbrush. Some might say that these added demands deterred misbehavior, but I disagree. These demands amounted to child abuse. I did not glean any fundamental truths, insights, or lessons from these demands.

We were often punished in other ways too. The staff members would often prevent us from enjoying a movie night. They could confine us in our rooms, suspend our use of appliances, restrict us from using the phone, or put us in the corner. They could apply these punishments at any moment and for any reason. If a staff member determined that he or she did not like you, things could get extremely harsh. I witnessed staff members placing kids in the corner for hours or confining them to their rooms for months. Sometimes, they would do this for insane and ridiculous reasons. The atmosphere was incredibly oppressive. Kids had to maintain a fake, upbeat, and jovial air of bravado. We had to maintain happy expressions at all times. This was unrealistic and downright impossible. What child can maintain a jovial attitude while suffering the most traumatic experience of his or her life? None can. Such onerous requirements were at best counterproductive and at worst child abuse. These tactics had no logical place in the sensitive environment of a group home.

These were the formal punishments; the informal punishments were completely different. There was a standing order in the group home to use force when necessary. They were allowed to use force against adolescents, preteens, and teenagers. This was not some rare practice either. At least once a week, they would use force, and they would do so at their own discretion. They would swiftly and violently take us down and then pin us to the ground. They used this practice whenever children were disruptive, out-of-control, verbally abuse, assaultive, or otherwise belligerent. The flaw of this practice was that the staff members were able to use their own discretion. A child might scream, "I hate it here! I want to go home!" This child might then go into his room and shut his bedroom door. For doing this, the staff members might deem him too disruptive, out-of-control, or verbally abusive. They would then take this child down by force. It was repugnant to witness, and I still have nightmares about it.

There was no uniform application of force either. Taking down offending children was each staff member's prerogative. As you can imagine, this varied from mild takedowns to outright assaults. On numerous occasions, I observed staff members palming a child's neck or head and smashing them violently to the ground. They would twist the child's wrist and trip him. They would hit the child in the back of the head and use their momentum to take the child down. These were the few takedowns I noticed or personally experienced. Another excruciating aspect was the duration of the restraint. The staff members might pin a child to the ground for hours. They might keep them pinned down until they deemed the child to be compliant. Children would cry and scream in agony for hours about the weight of grown adults crushing them. The staff members would pin them in awkward positions, which routinely caused their limbs to fall asleep. Takedowns are extremely exhausting. The physical, emotional, and mental toll is immeasurable. If a given takedown were warranted, then it might be tolerable, but the takedowns were rarely warranted. Whether intentionally or inadvertently, the male staff members would perversely derive sexual pleasure from these takedowns. It was not uncommon for a man to get aroused through forcibly pinning an innocent preteen to the ground. It was so common that we even had a name for it: *foody*. This term was a combination of *force* and *woody*. It was an extremely degrading experience. It was revolting to have a staff member's erect penis imprinted on your back or your buttocks.

Adjusting to this new environment was a constant struggle. I was accustomed to being free, outspoken, and inquisitive. At the group home, I felt oppressed. They were treating me harshly and forcing me to comply with a totalitarian regime. My nature was at odds with the group home immediately. No matter how hard I tried to assimilate, it seemed like I could never do my tasks or chores right. I struggled to maintain an upbeat jovial attitude. My bed wasn't tight enough. I had not dried some of the dishes properly. I vacuumed the floors too slowly. Their reprimands and punishments added up quickly. Within weeks, I was either confined to my room or completing chores. The other kids suffered the same fate. It was a small consolation that I was not alone, but life quickly became unbearable. I received some reprieve when I was enrolled at Cascade Middle School for the seventh grade. School became a haven where I could leave my troubles behind. I met new people and found joy in my schoolwork. I also met Charlotte at this school. Charlotte was in the same grade as me. She was extremely nice, warmhearted, and attractive. She became my shoulder to lean on and my confidant. I confided in her about my troubles at the group home and the heartache that I felt about my mother abandoning me. She listened attentively and encouraged me. To this day, I appreciate her kindness.

Living at the group home became such a hardship. I was at a fragile point in my life. I had just turned thirteen and I was going through puberty. I was trying to cope with my abandonment issues. To say the least, I was an emotional roller coaster. I would be feeling up one minute and down the next minute. It was hard on me. I failed to connect to any of the staff members. Only one staff member, John, even came close to connecting with me. John had an easy smile. He was a big guy. He was about six feet and two inches tall, and he weight about 220 pounds. He was not as critical as the rest of the staff members, and he would kindly be satisfied with your chores if he knew you had worked hard. He would not punish or reprimand anyone unjustly. These attributes were rare among the faculty. The other boys and I gravitated toward him more than any of the other staff members. His soft-spoken nature was welcoming. He would consistently dispense positive words of comfort, consolation, encouragement, and affection. It was as if he actually cared for us. He would go out of his way to talk to me, see me, and humor me. Occasionally, he would bring me candy bars, pop, and snacks. Candy and junk food was a delicacy at the group home. They did not offer or condone it. To have candy or junk food was a hidden pleasure. I would rush off with it as if it were gold. I would hide it in my closet so that no other staff members would see me eating it. Eventually, I took John's kindness as genuine. The rest of the faculty members were strict, impersonal, and intimidating. However, I did have some reservations about John. His soft-spoken demeanor and his subtle gestures subconsciously raised some red flags, though I did not know why. For instance, when I walked into a room, he would watch me closely and not say anything. I could tell that he was thinking about something that involved me, but he never divulged what he was thinking. Other things bothered me too. He would sometimes leave his hand on me for an uncomfortably long amount of time, or he'd remark about my body in some weird way. He would tell me that my legs looked good when I was wearing shorts, or he'd asked if I was growing hair yet under my arms and crotch. I did not like this sort of attention, but I did like his kindness. So, I shrugged off my concerns. I assumed that I was wrong to question him.

My days at the group home went by slowly, but my time at school seemed to fly by. Going to school was a pleasure; being at the group home was a pain. Before I knew it, I had been in the group home for three months. The months did nothing but exacerbate my longing to go home to my mother and brother. I never felt like I had settled in. The group home maintained an air of institutional sanitization. Each kid had his own hygiene products that he had to keep in his bedroom cabinet. There were no toys or personal possessions lying around. Everything was manicured and sanitized. It was hell. How do you get comfortable in a setting like that? As with hospitals, mental institutions, and prisons, you never feel fully adjusted. My problems began as they had for all of the kids. The chores, rules, punishments, and penalties were a labyrinth of potholes. I'd step out of one and then into another. I never seemed to have free time to read or do anything. I was always working, and I just got tired of it. I started rebelling. I started questioning their authority. They weren't my parents. I didn't care about them enough to listen to them, so I ignored them. In a group home that exploits children, this was unacceptable. They couldn't let children get away with rebelling and refusing to do their work. First, they tried to punish me by assigning me more work. They quickly realized that since I wasn't doing my original chores, I definitely wouldn't do the added ones. They were right. Then they stopped me from watching movies on movie nights. They took my phone, confined me to my room, and suspended my use of appliances, but I shrugged these punishments off. I would defiantly sit in my room with a book. I liked this a lot more than being ordered around like a slave. That's what I felt like: a slave. I had been condemned to involuntary servitude.

When their punishments proved ineffective, they found one that was highly effective. They began devising excuses to use force against me. The first time it happened, I was in my room. I was oblivious to the oncoming onslaught. They kicked it off by opening my door and demanding that I do some outside chores. As usual, I declined. Rather than being argumentative, violent, or belligerent, I was respectful.

The next thing I knew, the staff member yelled, "Clear the floor." This was code for the impending use of force. I tried to argue that my behavior did not merit the use of force. I extended my arms out in front of me to ward him off. My voice betrayed my fright. Nothing I could say or do would stop him. He came charging at me and clotheslined me, knocking me down to the ground. My nose and lips were bleeding immediately from the hard blow. Lying on the ground, he fell on me heavily. His weight took my breath away. Roughly, he turned me around so that my chest was facing the ground. My body was splayed out, and both of my arms were to my side.

Out of nowhere, more staff members came in and jumped on

me. I couldn't believe they were doing this. I posed no immediate threat. I was not being insolent, verbally abusive, assaultive, or otherwise belligerent. I knew what warranted force, and I did not meet that criteria. Their elbows dug into my flesh, and their fingernails punctured my skin. Four staff members were on top of me. There were three men and there was one woman. I was struggling to breathe. Then they started raising their demands.

"We're not going to let you go until you comply," said one of the staff members.

"Are you going to comply?" said another.

"We'll stay here all day if you don't," said the third male when I did not immediately respond to the second male's question.

"Daniel, you know it will be a lot easier on you if you comply," said the female staff member.

"Yes. I will comply," I grunted breathlessly.

"Are you going to start doing your chores, penalties, and punishments now?" asked the male staff member who had initially taken me down. Under this pressure, the minutes felt like hours. I had been struggling for a little more than an hour. I was exhausted. The struggle had zapped every ounce of energy from me.

"Yes. I will. I promise. I will. I will. Please let me go," I begged through the tears and the exhaustion.

"OK. But you know what's going to happen if you don't comply, right?" the first staff member whispered in my ear. "You're going to be hurting worse than this, I promise."

I did not doubt him. His threats were real. He had the power and the inclination to invent reasons to use force against me. They might not allow staff members to spank or beat us, but they would surely allow them to use force. Some of the staff members clearly had no problem using force as a punishment rather than a last resort. It was a despicable practice. I could understand that they would need to use force if a child posed an immediate threat, but to use force in such a brutal and unwarranted way was wrong. The staff members had the opportunity to harm children into submission. It was really assault.

After the first assault, I withdrew more into myself. I completed my chores fretfully. I was scared like an abused dog or a woman who is the victim of domestic abuse. I got nervous whenever certain staff members came near me. I kept my head down subserviently. I was too scared to look anyone in the eyes. I exhibited all of the signs of a downtrodden soul. They had won. I couldn't defeat them. I was easy fodder for them to twist into submission.

By acquiescing to their chores and added penalties, I temporarily made myself less visible to them. Other kids were taking the spotlight. There was always someone garnering the ire of the staff members who gained pleasure from dispensing harsh penalties. No kids were immune to this mistreatment. They treated all of the kids equally. Penalties and punishments were a way of life for us. On certain days, our punishments would be more pronounced. It seemed like the staff members were intent on making our time there unbearable.

One could argue that the use of force was warranted the second time I was assaulted, but I maintain that it was uncalled for. It started with a phone call. Charlotte had called to talk to me. I had expected her call, and I had given the faculty notice. They gave me permission to use the phone for half an hour. Talking to Charlotte was my only outlet. I never received calls from anyone else. Everyone else had forgotten me. I was alone, and Charlotte was the only one I wanted to talk to. She lent me her sympathetic ear, and I looked forward to our conversations. I heard the phone ring, and I walked briskly to the office. When someone calls for a resident, staff members typically put a chair outside the office door and then set the phone down next to the resident. On this particular day, John was manning the office. I eagerly stood in the doorway and listened to him answer the phone and use Charlotte's name. I was chomping at the bit to chat with her. I was getting those butterflies I occasionally got when I talked to her. Instead of following protocol, John seemed to be verbally engaging her. I struggled to hear what he was saying.

"Hello. Who is speaking?" John asked. "Oh, hi Charlotte. I'm sorry. You cannot speak to Daniel. He already used up his time on the phone with his girlfriend, Angela."

I ran into the office and yelled, "He's lying, Charlotte! I don't even know an Angela! He's a liar!"

"I'm sorry you had to hear about Daniel's girlfriend through me," John said hurriedly. With his hands outstretched, he pushed me back so that I could not get to the phone.

"He's lying! Don't believe him," I yelled.

"OK, bye," John said as he hung up the phone.

I could not believe John would do something like this. He was the one staff member who had been kind and gentle, but he was trying to destroy the one meaningful relationship that I had. His conversation with Charlotte had been laced with animosity and a touch of jealousy.

"Why did you do that?" I demanded.

"Don't worry about it," he responded with anger in his eyes. "She's just a tramp who would break your heart anyway."

"No she's not!" I screamed. I ran down to my room, found Charlotte's phone number in my address book, and ran back to the office. Discarding the rules and ignoring John's authority, I went into the office, grabbed the phone, and started to dial her number.

"You're not allowed to be in here," John blurted.

I was beyond listening to him. All I could think about was Charlotte. I no longer cared about the nice and kind things John had done for me.

"Clear the floor!" John yelled.

I looked at him with deep fury. I kept uselessly trying to dial the number, knowing that at any moment they were going to take me down. Then it happened. John grabbed my neck. He tried to pull me to the ground, but he only managing to get me into a headlock. I struggled against him violently, angry that he would be so cruel. More staff members materialized, and they successfully took me to the ground. I was only a skinny thirteen-year-old. I couldn't resist them.

John and the other staff members were on top of me, and I screamed in agony. John had his full weight on me. The other two held my legs and arms. It was hard to breathe. I felt like I was suffocating again.

"Are you going to calm down?" John said. His lips came revoltingly close to my ear. I could feel his ragged, hot breath exhaling and inhaling. The inappropriateness of his contact with me just fueled my anger.

"Get off of me! I hate you! I hate this place!" I screamed. The verbal explosion provoked them to tighten and strengthen their grip.

"Calm down, Daniel," John said with a touch of pleasure.

To my horror, John was getting pleasure from being on top of me. He continued to breathe into my ear like he was feeling stimulated. Unknown to the other staff members, John was slowly rubbing his erect penis on my backside. This disgusting motion repelled me violently, giving me a second wind of resistance as I twisted and turned beneath their grip. My struggles were worthless, though. They just held on harder and handled me more roughly.

The only way to escape was to sheepishly calm down. Mentally, this was the last thing that I wanted to do. I would have liked to punch John's lights out, but I couldn't do that. He was in charge here. He had the power of a posse behind him. My best bet was to get out of this situation and then stay the hell away from John.

Finally, they relented. They let up and allowed me to pull myself off of the ground. The struggle had caused all of my energy to evaporate. I limped to my room, fell on my bed, and passed out immediately. I went to school the next day with one thing in mind. I had to talk to Charlotte. I had to explain the situation and tell her about John's cruelty, malice, and perverseness. When I saw her, I withheld some of the facts. I could not divulge the full extent of John's depravity, but I shared enough information with her and she believed me. She said that she had been certain all along that I would never see another girl behind her back.

When I returned to the group home, I quietly did my chores. I knew that I had to stay away from John, so I remained as busy as possible. I did everything in my power to not be in the same room as him. When he would enter a room, I would exit it. If he asked me to do some task or chore, I would silently comply, but I did not engage in any conversation with him. I did not maintain any eye contact or project any friendliness. He knew that I didn't want anything to do with him, and I hoped that he would steer clear of me.

I had come to a crucial realization after the incident with John. I recognized the signs for what they were. John was kind, gentle, and soft-spoken. He brought me candy and junk food in violation of the rules of the group home. He had been grooming me, just like he had probably been grooming the other kids. He had been trying to win my trust and help me feel secure with him. He was a disgusting predator who was waiting for the right time to make his move.

Even though I had discovered the truth about John, I had no clue what to do about it. I still was under the care of the group home. Unless I obtained permission, I had no access to a phone. I did not get along or feel comfortable with any of the other staff members. Even if I had told the other staff members about John's secret, they would not have believed me. They'd say I made it up. They'd say it was a figment of my overactive imagination. There was no formal procedure for filing a complaint. If there had been, I still would have lacked the mental acuity to articulate my suspicions. I was too scared, embarrassed, and insecure to voice my concerns to adults, so I tried to forget about it. But

I did not forgive him or try to befriend him again. I just tried my hardest to stay away from him. I tried to forget that he even existed. In my book, he didn't deserve to exist. It was deplorable for him to prey on young, emotionally scarred kids who had been discarded. He was a freak. No matter how hard I tried to avoid John, I could not escape him. He perceived me as a challenge, and he pursed me intently. Weeks had gone by since the phone incident. In the interim, he had apologized profusely. He had wailed about how he had been stressed out. He came to work each day with candy and junk food. I consistently refused to take anything from him, but this did not stop him. He would sneak into my room and put it under my pillow or in my dresser. Nothing I said or did dissuaded his fixation, but I remained steadfast in my conviction. His soft and gentle words fell on deaf ears. I would not intentionally invite any attention from him. I'd be cordial, but that was all. John's fixation with me finally manifested itself physically. His silent stalking campaign ended. My attempts at ignoring him only bolstered his sick fantasies. To him, my evasiveness was a tacit sign that I welcomed his advances.

After school one day, I returned to the group home and went up to my room. I threw my backpack on the bed and then went about my chores while listening to music on my Walkman. At this point, I had gotten into a routine. I knew what the group home wanted from me. The daily ritual had become second nature. I could not always get through my chores and routine unscathed, though. I would occasionally rankle a staff member's feathers, but I did my best not to disturb anyone. I knew my place. I knew that they could take me down if I got out of line, so I kept my mouth shut and did whatever they told me to do. This was their house, and I had nowhere else to go. No one wanted me. I could either stay there or live on the streets, so I chose to stay there. Then it happened. It was so devastating that I completely reversed my decision to stay there.

The evening went by swiftly. My last duty was to clean the bathroom downstairs. I was supposed to clean it at the end of the night, when all of the other children were getting into bed upstairs. That way, it would be clean for the next day. There was nothing unusual about this chore. As usual, the whole bottom floor was empty, and all the staff members and kids were upstairs. I had my cleaning supplies in hand, and I was busily scrubbing the toilet and the surrounding area. I did not hear anyone enter the bathroom. I was oblivious to the intruder. He stood silently behind me, watching me work. It was not until he turned the water on in the sink that I realized he was there. Shocked, I stood up immediately and dropped my scrubbing pad.

"What do you want, John?" I asked nervously.

"Oh, I was just enjoying the sight," he stated inappropriately. "I've been meaning to tell you something."

"Well, I'm busy," I said. "Just tell me tomorrow."

"No. I've held this in for long enough," he replied. "I've got feelings for you, Daniel. I think I love you."

"You're crazy!" I stated. "Get away from me!" I tried to push past him and get through the door, but it was impossible. John was too big and too strong. He easily grabbed me. With the water still running, our sounds were muffled.

"Calm down. If you scream, I'm going to take you down. Then I'll hurt you," he said with his sick lips against my ear. "I just want to make you feel good."

"No, please! Just leave me alone," I begged.

"It will be all right," he whispered in my ear. "You're going to like it."

"No, I won't!" I protested. Then he exposed himself, pulling his manhood out disgustingly. Once it was out, he proceeded to put his hands down my pants and fondle my penis. I violently struggled under his embrace. I was panicking. I did not know what to do. John's brazen acts had taken me by surprise. The situation was overloading my senses. John persisted to molest me, repulsively kissing my neck and ears while I squirmed under him. His actions proceeded unabated until someone finally saved me. A male staff member was yelling for John. Thank God. I had been rescued from this madman. He hurriedly pulled up his pants.

"This is between us. If you tell anyone else, they won't believe you anyway. And then I'll hurt you. In more ways than one," said John with a mean expression. "Promise me now that you won't say nothing." He bunched my shirt up into his fist.

"OK. I won't say nothing," I said with fear in my eyes.

Then John went into the hallway and then up into the office. I left the cleaning supplies where they were. I rushed to my room, got in bed, threw the covers over my head, and nervously peeked out, monitoring the bedroom door in fear. I stayed up for most of the night. Sleep was elusive. How could I sleep? I was incredibly afraid for my safety. I had not anticipated John's actions. I had had an idea about his deviancy, but I never believed he would try to force himself on me. If I had come to this realization, I would have taken more precautions. I would have been more vigilant.

Every shadow that passed by my bedroom door sent shivers down my spine. By the time breakfast had come, I was a nervous wreck. I was surprised that no one noticed how awful I felt. If they had noticed, though, why would they have cared? Amazingly, not one staff member showed a remote interest in me, but the other kids noticed that something was wrong. My roommate could tell that something was wrong. My normal countenance was gone. I looked fearful and uneasy, but I tried to play it off and act nonchalantly. I'm certain my roommate recognized the warning signs. He could tell that I had been abused, molested, and defiled.

I did not share my experience with the other kids or the adults. My childhood logic felt clear. If I told anyone, he or she would not believe me. He or she would tell my perpetrator what I had said, and this would trigger painful reprisals. My own experiences and my knowledge of the faculty supported this conclusion. The staff members looked at us as wards and juvenile delinquents. They did not see us as innocent kids. Clearly, they were only loyal to each other. Children just passed through this group home. We would grace the group home temporarily and inconsequentially. We were a paycheck and that was it. I had known this from the moment I had been dragged through the front door. If I were to have openly accused John of molesting me, they would have circled the wagons. They would have found reasons to disbelieve me. They would have painted me as a liar. There was no way I was going through that.

For days afterward, I thought nonstop about my situation. What was I going to do? Could I ever feel safe here? Were the other kids safe here? Should I think of them or should I just think about myself? Should I sneak away in the night? I thought about trekking for many miles until I reached civilization. I could then get on a bus and leave. But where would I go? Could I take the other kids with me? We could depend on each other for survival. I didn't know what to do. I felt bewildered. I was only sure of one thing: I had to escape. Otherwise, I would never be safe. Leaving was my only viable option.

John was infinitely more frightening when he sexually assaulted me than the priest had been. I knew John. He had at one point gained my trust. It was extremely frightening to see him after he had abused me. Through his mean expressions, he conveyed silent warnings that paralyzed me, but his attempts to be nice were even worse. These fake attempts just highlighted his deceptiveness. How he could play this role? How could he act as if nothing had happened? It was maddening. He knew that he had power over me. This was his house. I could not escape further abuse from him. It was only a matter of time before he would attack me again. I was going to flee with the others or by myself. It was the only choice I had.

CHAPTER 4

Once I was determined to run away, I had to figure out how to go about it. I did not plan my first attempt very well. There was no preparation and no plan. I was highly motivated to free myself from this nightmare, but motivation wasn't enough. I needed to think things out more. I had to foresee the consequences of my actions. More importantly, I had to anticipate my necessities. I needed directions on where to go, how to get there, and what resources were needed.

My first attempt was a wild dash to freedom. I spent the day explaining, detailing, and describing my plan to the other kids. I explained how hard it was living here. I explained how we would be better off on our own. It was not a hard sell. All of the kids hated it there. It was unnecessary to devise a colorful presentation. What was needed was a visionary. We needed someone who could paint the picture. By default I was this person. I did not necessarily want to be in this position. It was not in my natural disposition to become the salesman for our exodus, but I did not want to leave the other kids behind to be further abused, molested, and raped. I had to do something. Taking our safety into our own hands seemed like the only remedy. I wanted to control our destinies. I did not want to allow some pedophile and an abusive staff to dictate our destinies for us.

After explaining the reasons we had to escape, I had to get down to the details. I thought that we should leave immediately and get the hell away from that place. None of us were safe there. I told them that we would have to do more chores if we waited. We would be punished and exploited more if we stayed any longer. I still could not share the real truth. Staying there meant that we might possibly be sexually abused. At any point in time, John could corner one of them and rape them. Maybe I should have explained the seriousness of the situation, but I could not find the courage to do so. I could not overcome my shame and embarrassment. I told myself that the next best thing was to get them all out of there.

After we all agreed to leave immediately, there was a flurry of activity. All of the kids at Auburn Group Home gathered their belongings together. We had a variety of big duffel bags, suitcases, and backpacks. Between the six of us, we had twelve bags. We did not think about how hard it would be to walk for miles with these heavy bags. We did not think about how the heavy bags would hinder us. We just wanted to escape with our possessions so that we could start our new lives together. We wanted to be free from the constraints of oppression and abuse.

We left after dinner. We did not bring any food, water, or money, but we did have our clothes, our hygiene products, and our toys. Yes, some of us still had toys. No matter how the staff viewed us, we were still kids. We still had a sense of imagination. This sense of imagination and wishful thinking might have been what enabled us to flee. Each kid considered how our escape would unfold. Regretfully, imagination doesn't get you very far in the real world.

With six hyper kids eagerly packing their belongings, it did not take long for the staff to catch onto what we were doing. Amazingly, however, no staff members tried to stop us. They gave us no verbal warnings. It seemed strange and almost unreal that they were so dispassionate and uncaring. They did not even have the decency to warn us about real threats. They didn't tell us that someone might kidnap us or wild animals might attack us. We might die of dehydration or starvation. They just let us walk out the door, loaded down with our bags. We were so unprepared. It was ridiculous. Within an hour of leaving early that evening, most of us were exhausted. The journey had taken its toll. At first, the euphoria propelled us onward. We joked and played around. We stuck mostly to the winding country roads. But when we passed a cow pasture with three lines of barbwire around it, we momentarily strayed into it. While in the pasture I remember jokingly challenging Mike to tip over a cow. We maintained a sense of community. We felt like we were going to be all right. We were blazing a path, but the initial excitement soon wore off. The sun went down and evening crept in. Then night came. We started to fight. Some of the kids whined about being scared, thirsty, and unsure of themselves. We saw bats dipping down among us, and this added to our fears.

By the second hour, everybody except for me wanted to go back. Their need for freedom had been sated. Loudly, they expressed their concerns.

"Let's go back. We're never going to survive like this. We don't have food, water, or money," one of them would say.

"Yeah, this was stupid. Let's go back," another one would readily agree. The tone of the expedition had changed dramatically. I tried arguing venomously in favor of continuing on our journey.

"We can't go back. This is our only hope!" I explained.

"If we go back we will regret it."

"No we won't. At least we'll have a roof over our heads and food to eat," one of the kids retorted.

"Yeah, but you'll be living in misery and worked tirelessly. Plus, we'll be severely punished for running away," I argued desperately. "Trust me, this is the best option. Otherwise, we'll hate ourselves for giving up."

"I won't hate myself. I'm already used to getting punished anyway. More punishment isn't a big deal," one of the kids declared solemnly.

The tide had changed. Kids who had once been ardent supporters were now vocal opponents. They were tired of walking and they wanted to go back. United, they all were against trekking onward.

"Who cares about the punishment?" they would ask. It was a losing battle. Even Mike, my closest friend, expressed his doubts.

"Daniel, we can't make it like this. We did not think this out properly," he said with regret.

"I am with you 100 percent. I hate it there too, but we've got to do it right!"

"This will turn out all right!" I argued.

"You don't know that. Anything could happen to us," he said softly. "Let's go back, reevaluate our plans, and then go from there. If we come up with a better plan we can try again."

"I don't think I can spend another night in that place," I stated emotionally.

"Why? Is there something you're not telling me?" Mike asked intuitively.

"No," I said quickly. "I am just miserable there. I miss my family so much."

"I know. So do I," he said, putting his arm around my shoulder. "We can be each other's family from now on."

"Yeah. I'd like that," I said, wiping a tear away. "So, are you serious about running away with me again?"

"Yes, I will," he said, smiling. "But we'll have to do it right."

"All right. Let's go back," I said reluctantly.

Once Mike and I had privately made our pact, we gave in to

the general plan of returning to the nightmare voluntarily. I was not happy about it, but I was scared to go on alone. I was fearful that it would be unsafe for me to wander around the world alone, so we turned back and retraced our steps. Arriving back at the group home, we received no solace and nothing even remotely close to peace. All I felt was apprehension, fear, and nervousness. I was returning voluntarily to the place of my nightmares. It was hard to take. All of my senses told me to run away, but I was still a child. I was unsure of myself. I lacked the confidence to assertively dismiss the notion of returning. If I did not return, though, I would have to travel the road alone. I was not ready for that yet. I still needed to gain more confidence. Deep down I felt like unwanted trash. How can garbage survive by itself? I needed someone. Staying was not an option, yet leaving by myself was scary. I found consolation in the fact that I was returning temporarily. I knew that Mike and I would run away together and survive on our own.

Unsurprisingly, the group home had not called the police or Child Protective Services. Nobody. They had filed no reports about our four-hour peregrination. Our absence did not seem to bother them. Nobody was on high alert. They would just fill the beds with a new load of foster kids. We could have been injured, abducted, or mauled by wild animals; it didn't matter to them.

We arrived at the front door to find it locked. The staff members had seen no reason to leave it unlocked for us. After pounding on the door and ringing the doorbell, we waited. Ten minutes went by. They could hear and see us. They just wanted to drag the process out. The lady answered the door reluctantly.

"What do you want?" she asked haughtily.

"We decided to come back," Mike said assuredly.

"How do you know I'll let you back in?" she asked rudely. "I don't have to let you back in, you know."

"OK. We're sorry. We won't do it again," someone said. At the moment, I was hoping that she would not let us in. I wanted her to force us to embark on our journey again.

"All right. But go straight back to your rooms," she said sternly.

"OK," we said in unison.

While going up the stairs, someone said, "You guys don't care about any of us, do you?"

"No. Why should we?" the woman asked seriously. Remarkably, this uncaring woman was pregnant. Her unborn baby had not instilled any compassion in her.

"You don't have to be rude about it," one of the kids replied.

"I'm not being rude. I'm just stating a fact," she said vindictively.

"Screw you! You're a jerk!" one of the kids declared childishly.

Returning to my bedroom, I fitfully tried to sleep. Tossing and turning, I began contemplating my next move. I realized that walking out of the group home was no longer an option. The long walk was too tiresome. It required too much energy. The best solution would be to run away from the city. I could take buses from the city of Auburn to Seattle. Our starting point needed to be in the city. Disregarding the normal protocol of allowing us to gradually get up, the morning staff members woke us all up abruptly the next morning.

"Wake up! Wake up!" a male staff member yelled loudly, banging a metal spoon against a big pot for added emphasis. "Be downstairs in the living room in five minutes or there will be hell to pay!"

All of the kids woke up violently and rushed into their clothes like firemen. My roommate and I exchanged nervous glances. We knew there was going to be some reckoning. There was no way around it. We hoped that they would not be too severe, but this was just wishful thinking.

Once we had all gathered downstairs, the staff members began their diatribe. Their position was clear. They were angry, but we could not figure out why. The staff did not care about us. They didn't seem to care whether we stayed or left. Why were they emanating such rage with their fiery eyes? The staff members were reacting as if we had personally affronted them. This puzzled me. With a loud slap on the coffee table, the same tall man that dragged me from my mom's car opened the meeting. His face was red with pent-up fury. The other two staff members silently supported him as he took the floor.

"What you did yesterday was completely unacceptable," He growled. "Your behavior is inexcusable." Turning his attention to my roommate, he said, "Look at me when I'm talking to you, boy!" He leaned over the coffee table and grabbed Mike's face with one hand. "Things are going to change around here. We have been too nice to you, and what did we get for our kindness? Shit." He said. Walking around the room glaring at us, he spat. "Mostly, you will be punished for your mistreatment of a pregnant staff member." We had solved the puzzle. They were angry about what some of the kids had said in that moment of self-conscious childishness. The kids had not been threatening, malicious, or angry, yet the staff members acted this way toward us.

The punishments that they gave us were harsh but expected. We had to do loads of work. We were confined to our rooms, and they took our appliances away. Walkmans, radios, handheld video games, and fans were lugged to some unknown location. We had to write essays about how wrong we had been for running away and talking harshly to the pregnant staff member. We were not allowed to talk to each other for one week, and we had to eat alone in our rooms. We were completely isolated and it was nearly impossible to endure.

The hours of work and confinement, however, gave me the time to plan my escape. I had to decide which resources to bring and which route to take. I could not risk failing again. Staying at the group home was dangerous. Every day was a battle to refrain from running and hiding every time John entered a room. It was a battle to not vomit from the fright. I did not know when John might strike next. I took extremely cautionary steps to avoid him, but every step I took highlighting his power over me. I hated him for that. I hated how he had lowered me to the level of being a victim who was forced to cower away from his perpetrator. I was not just avoiding him occasionally; I avoided him five days a week. His shifts became an obstacle course. I watched my steps as if landmines might explode at any moment. It was terrible. My memories of those days are unimaginably painful.

The escape plan was simple. We would go to school with our backpacks filled with the bare necessities: water bottles, stolen food, two changes of clothes, and hygiene products. We would then board a bus to Seattle. Mike had procured twenty dollars that we could use for our expenditures. We would go back to my home, and I would explain the situation to my mom. I would describe the sexual abuse that I had experienced. I would express the direness of our circumstances, and she would undoubtedly do the right thing. She would allow me to stay with her, and I hoped that she would let my friend Mike stay too.

Because of my heightened sense of anticipation, the morning of the great escape came at a drudging pace. The anticipation was particularly clear on my face, which radiated a glow of hopefulness. I gained immense pleasure from my knowledge that I would soon be free of this nightmare. The only thing that had made my days bearable was the thought of this day. I thought often about how I would soon get rid of these endless feelings of pain and fear. In some ways, I believed that escaping my abuser would nullify the abuse that I had gone through. I thought that escaping would allow me to leave behind any memory of this awful experience. At the very least, I needed to escape the prospect of future abuse. This is what drove me and inspired me to throw my doubts to the wind.

As soon as the school bus arrived at school, Mike and I ran off of the school grounds. I had shared my plan with Charlotte the day before and said good-bye to her. I had promised that I would be in contact with her daily, and I had left it at that. There was no use guaranteeing future fidelity. My future was unclear and unpredictable. No matter how much I cared for her, I could not guarantee anything.

We found a bus that was bound for Seattle. We got on it and settled in, kicking our feet up luxuriously. We sent each other smiles of jubilation. The feeling was euphoric. We gradually forgot about the constraints of the group home. The threats of future abuse started to lift. We gave each other high fives. We had done it. Our journey felt like it would be easy sailing from then on. Nothing could stop us. The bus took us to downtown Seattle. From there we located a bus to take us to the north end of town: Greenwood. I couldn't wait to get home. It was not hard to find the right bus. The trip was even easier. It seemed like everything was flowing smoothly. By the time we arrived, it was noon. We stepped off the bus across the street from a convenience store on 85th and Aurora. From there, we walked straight up 85th. I knew this neighborhood like the back of my hand. It was delightful to see the familiar antique store, the McDonald's, and the Fred Meyer. It felt amazing. This was my homecoming. I had arrived.

It is hard to describe the feelings that these familiar surroundings evoked. Seeing the Blockbuster Video store reminded me of the day that it had opened. I had been there at the grand opening, which had included free popcorn, balloons, and someone walking around in a Teenage Mutant Ninja Turtle costume. We were allowed to get a free picture taken with him. I was probably eight years old, but I still remember it vividly. Up the street from the video store was Greenwood Elementary. I had attended this school during my last full year at home. I had been in the fifth grade. Walking up the street with Mike, I wished that I could go back to those days. It felt invigorating to pass these landmarks. They represented a happier time in my life.

They represented safety, contentment, and love.

When we were a few blocks from my house, I was no longer walking. My feelings of bliss carried me along as I glided home. Mike and I slung our arms over each other's shoulders. Laughing, we sang the song "We're off to see the Wizard" from *The Wizard of Oz*. Before arriving at the house, we hungrily consumed our sandwiches, chips, and water quickly as we walked. We had stolen enough food for two meals each. This should have been plenty. We only needed enough food to last us until we arrived at my house. Once we got there, we would worry about our next meal. If the house were the same as it had been when I had left, this would be a valid concern, but we could cross that bridge when we got there.

Turning the corner of my old street, we headed toward my childhood home. It soon became visible. I almost dropped to my knees with elation. My smile broadly expanded across my face. I felt exhilarated. Then my smile slowly faded. I indented my eyebrows inquisitively. Something was different. There was a new mailbox, and a new wooden landing for the front door. I had never seen the cars that were parked out before. I tried to believe that these differences meant nothing. I tried to convince myself that my mother and my brother still lived there, but the evidence kept piling up against me. Infant toys were lying around. The yard had been mown and there were flowers in the garden. I didn't want to believe what I was seeing, but I knew that my mom never planted flowers, and she was too old to have a newborn.

"What's wrong? Isn't this your house?" Mike asked, putting his hand on my shoulder.

"Yes. It is," I said, "But it looks like someone else lives here now."

"What do you mean? Your mom wouldn't sell the house and move without telling you," he said nervously. "Would she?"

I could not answer him. I wanted to defend my mother for

moving without telling me, but I could not do it. Instead of answering his question, I walked up to the door. I knocked on the familiar dark wood and rang the doorbell. I had a flashback of a happier time, when I was nine and playing a joke on my brother, David. I had run out the sliding glass door, and I had gone around to the front door, where I rang the doorbell and laughed. Since my parents were deaf, they had a light connected to the doorbell that would blink on and off. As a prank, I would ring it and then run back inside. I thought that this was very funny, especially when my older brother would run to find out who was doing this. They knew that I was the one who did this. This particular time, my brother acted like he was returning to his bedroom. Then he hid and waited for me to do it again. I crept around to the front door and rang the doorbell again. Then I ran back to the sliding glass door. You can imagine my shock when I saw my brother standing there with the door locked. He was laughing and waving at me.

I was not laughing when I saw the woman from India open the door. I was shocked. Secretly, I had still been hoping that I was wrong and that my mom still lived there. The sight of this unknown person in my house confirmed my fears.

"Hello. Can you tell me what happened to the deaf lady who used to live here?" I asked.

"Yes. She moved two months ago," the woman said haltingly. "I buy. It good house."

"You would not happen to know her address, would you?" I asked hopefully.

"No. Not know. I have mail for her. Not know were to send it," she said honestly.

"OK. Thank you for your time. Bye," I said as I walked away crying.

I tried to hide my tears, wiping them away quickly so that Mike wouldn't see them. I wanted to appear tough, but inside I was torn up. My hopes had been dashed. I would not find shelter here. My mother had sold the house, and she had not told me. The one place that I had felt would always be there was now gone. It was no longer my home. I went from happiness to desperation. I did not know what to do. I knew that I would never go back to that group home voluntarily. That was not an option, but I did not want to be homeless either. The thought of being homeless was scary. What else could I do?

"Now what are we going to do?" Mike asked. "We have to figure something out before nightfall. I can't sleep outside!"

"I don't know," I said. "Let me think."

I walked down the block and sat down on a curb.

"Do you know anywhere we can go?" I asked.

"No," he said sadly. Mike had nobody to turn to either. The difference, however, was that he accepted the fact that his parents did not want him. I, on the other hand, was still in denial. I still harbored the belief the government or some unknown entities were keeping me apart from my family. No amount of contrary evidence could convince me otherwise. Maybe I should have been like Mike. Perhaps then I would not have been so crushed in situations like this. My hopes had been high in the sky, but they had fallen drastically to the ground, where they shattered into a million pieces.

We walked up the street to Sandel Park and sat on a bench that I had sat on countless times during my adolescence. It faced the basketball court that David had schooled me on. This was the park where I used to play Cops and Robbers, football, and basketball. It was one block from my old house, and it encompassed a full city block. It had a jungle gym, a swing set, and a kiddie pool that wasn't more than three feet deep. Every summer the city reopened it, inviting all of the neighborhood kids to frolic and play in it. The park also had a summer lunch program. They provided sack lunches and sponsored fun activities, such as roller-skating and playing tag and hide-and-go-seek. They also had a slip-and-slide. Parents loved it too because they could leave their kids there while school was out. Every summer this went down like clockwork.

The lunch program, though, was not running today. It would not be running for two more months. Our food reserve was wholly inadequate. Our two meals had dwindled down to one. By the time night fell, we had no more meals left. We walked to the houses of some of my old friends and asked if they knew where my mother had moved. None of them knew. They were more interested in knowing why I had run away and what the group home had been like. Tony, one of my childhood friends, gave me some leftovers from dinner. I split them with Mike. None of my old friends offered to shelter us. It was a school night, and their parents wouldn't let us stay with them, so we continued to roam around the vicinity of my old house. I felt like I was tethered to my old house like a forlorn spirit, capturing safety and comfort from its closeness. We had no illusions, though; we were homeless. We could not wander around all night. There was no clear path to where we could lay our heads. The worn-down wooden bench offered very little comfort, but it was off of the ground. A small awning from the building that housed the lunch program would keep the cold rain off of us. Pulling our arms into our shirts, we gathered warmth from our bodies. Our incessant shivering hindered us from sleeping well, but when dawn arrived we had gotten enough sleep to rise and face the world.

We were homeless. I would forever remember that night as my first night without a home. It would not be the last one, though. As I rose with the sun and saw the dew glistening on the grass, I felt an odd sense of empowerment. I had braved a night in the elements and slept on a bench. I had shivered my way through the worst that an April night could give me, and I had survived. This gave me confidence. If I could get through one night being homeless, I could get through many more nights. A newfound energy drove me onward. Mike seemed to feel somewhat better too. While we would have to suffer some discomfort in the cold, he too seemed to realize that we could survive. My ability to brave this hardship helped me feel empowered. I could dictate my own future and determine my own path in life. I was no longer at the whims of the adults who had abandoned me, ruled over me despotically, harmed me physically, or molested me sexually. I was my own captain, and I was free to navigate the world on my own terms. If adults mistreated me, they forfeited their rights to rule over me. I would no longer let them mistreat me.

With the sunny day before us, we traveled east toward Greenwood's town center. Once we arrived, we contrived a plan of action. We decided to panhandle, soliciting pedestrians as they left or entered neighboring shops. The big Safeway offered a key focal point from which we worked the commerce-driven street. Then we descended on the McDonald's, where we hungrily devoured our breakfast. The warm fodder and the warm interior nourished our weary bones. The restaurant was so welcoming that neither of us was in a rush to leave. Instead, we savored our food and allowed ourselves to enjoy the warmth. Our panhandling had added only one dollar to our dwindling resources. Our financial health was declining rapidly. Our initial twenty dollars had been reduced to ten dollar. With the addition of the dollar that we had panhandled, we were up to eleven dollars. We could not afford to purchase McDonald's again. In the future, we agreed to be frugal. We would need to stretch our funds to sustain us for as long as possible. With this financial austerity in place, we finally left in search of other ways to generate revenue.

We spent the whole day panhandling, amassing a sum of seven dollars. It was not a huge fortune, but it added beautifully to our eleven dollars. We purchased a loaf of bread, some meat, and some cheese. This became our lunch and dinner. We easily devoured the whole loaf. We were not thriving but we were surviving, and that was all that mattered. This was better than living in the group home. I missed school but I would not sacrifice my well-being to participate in it. I knew that if I went to school authorities they would probably send me back to the group home. I could not risk that. School was the only thing that I missed besides Charlotte, but even Charlotte could not make me want to suffer in the group home again. Maybe this was selfish, but I needed to focus on myself. How else would I remain mentally and physically intact?

By nightfall, we had found shelter in a newspaper bin. It was constructed out of wood, painted brown, and had the word "Newspapers" spray painted across the front. It was a newspaper recycling bin. It had a roof and four walls. Sure, there were two big slots through which people could throw newspapers in, but it was better than being exposed to the elements on the bench. If we covered the slots with garbage bags, we had additional protection. We might not have been cozy and warm, but it got us through the night relatively well. These were learning experiences for us. Finding adequate shelter was our highest priority. The newspapers also offered a softer pallet than the bench. It was bearable. Learning about different safe havens was crucial to our struggle to endure.

When I woke up on the second day, I was under attack. I had been hit in the face. The wallop had instantly woken me. I was disoriented, and the shock caused me to bolt me upright. Then I realized what was going on. Someone had thrown a stack of newspapers through the garbage bag covering the slots. The stack had hit me square in the face. It was quite the rude awakening. I tried to go back to sleep, but the blow and the new rush of cold air thwarted my efforts. Up until then, I had slept relatively well. Our body heat had warmed the interior sufficiently. With our body heat escaping, the temperature dropped precipitously, forcing me to face the morning. I jumped out and found a bush to water. By the time I got back, Mike was getting up.

With no planned agenda, we agreed to hit up the Safeway to purchase some low-cost breakfast supplies. With no place to cook anything meaningful, we settled on generic cereal and milk. Using an empty plastic container we had found, we took turns eating. Another night of homelessness was behind us. Food was in our bellies, and the sun was shining down on us. All was not great in our world, but it could have been worse.

Eating the bowl of cereal on the bench adjacent to Safeway, I started to put things into perspective. I remembered sitting on this exact bench selling items for my various school fundraisers. I would enlist Dennis to help me. We would go door-to-door until we reached the Safeway. Then we would set the items up in an area with a lot of traffic. The student who earned the most money would get a grand prize, and the other contenders would get smaller prizes. My competitive nature drove me to work hard and to sell more. I maintained a well-groomed appearance and I smiled a lot as I invited consumers to inspect my goods. My past appearance contrasted greatly with my current homeless appearance. The previous two days had added a layer of grime and dirt to my face and body. I looked filthy. The filmy ink from the newspapers had visibly rubbed off on me. I wondered about how pedestrians would react to me now. We immediately noticed the difference as we attempted to panhandle again on the second day. We did not have much luck, and we only managed to accrue a measly seventy cents. This was not even enough to cover the food we had purchased for breakfast, lunch, and dinner. I thought that our grungy appearance would advance our panhandling efforts, but I was wrong. People tended to shy away from us now. It was as if they were afraid that our grime might rub off on them. It was a galling experience.

Our funds had dwindled down to seven dollars, and we felt discouraged. The public had pointed out the flaw in our panhandling efforts. We were dependent on their generosity. If they felt uncharitable, we suffered. There had to be another way to generate revenue, but nothing became readily apparent. If America had not been so overly regulated, perhaps we could have found a job. Working at McDonald's would have been nice, but laws against child labor prevented us from doing this. The law stated that I had to be sixteen.

At nightfall we were blessed. As McDonald's was closing, we asked for their leftovers. They supplied us with a big bag full of hamburgers and fries. We were thrilled. Some of the bread was crusty and the fries were stale, but it was gourmet to us. We ate everything in one sitting, not even stopping to take a breath. We inhaled it all hungrily.

The food was not the only blessing we got. We also got a lead on where my mom and brother were. A guy I remembered from my old house gave it to us. His name was Ike, and he was one of David's friends. He also clued me in on some disturbing facts. He told me that my mom and David were staying in some apartments off of 105th and Aurora. That was a mere twenty blocks from my present location. I was elated. We could be there in half an hour. What he shared next bothered me immensely. He said that my mother had bought Ike a car for four thousand dollars. She had also bought an expensive purple Cadillac. She was blowing the money that she had made from selling the house. She had bought a car for a relative stranger, yet she had not sent me or my other siblings a dime. It felt absurd to learn about this.

We arrived at the apartment within twenty minutes. We rang the buzzer and waited patiently. No one answered. I looked for the purple Cadillac, but it was nowhere to be found. Next to the apartment's buzzer station it was parallel to the apartment, enclosing a neighboring vacant side yard waist-high wooden fence. We climbed over it and settled in as we awaited their return. About two hours went by. Then I heard the booming bass of a stereo exploding from an arriving car. It was the purple Cadillac. The sound system must have cost thousands of dollars. David hopped out of the car. I was so delighted to see him that I rushed over the fence and gave him a big hug. He was pleasantly shocked to see me too. He brought Mike and me up to the small one-bedroom apartment. My mom had been in there the whole time. She just could not hear the buzzer.

I explained the dire circumstances that had compelled me to escape the group home. I went into great detail about the abuse that I had suffered and the struggles that I had gone through to find them. My mother listened attentively. She did not berate me or condemn my actions, but she did not praise my endeavors either. She did not share her thoughts on the topic, but she told us to get into the shower. David gave Mike and I clean clothes to wear. I jumped in first, then Mike took a shower. The shower was invigorating. My mother offered us some food, but we both declined. We were still full from those leftovers. My mother set down some sheets and blankets on the floor for us to sleep on. We fell asleep immediately.

The next morning, I made everyone breakfast. I was extremely excited about being reunited with my family. I was beaming. I decided to surprise my mom with breakfast in bed. When she took the plate of eggs and bacon with toasted bread, she smiled to indicate her appreciation for it. I gratefully accepted her approval. I was hoping in some small way to ingratiate myself. Seeing her smile reminded me of a particularly warm moment from the past.

Only she and I had shared this moment. She was not the most physically active parent, but on this one occasion we dusted off her blue bicycle. It had a big basket on the handlebars. She had not ridden it in years. The two of us went on a bike ride. It was the first time we had ever done that. I peddled with ease up the streets of Seattle, while my mother strained to keep up. The hills of Seattle are famed for being mountainous and steep, and the route we had taken was leading to the steepest neighborhood. Our destination was the Little Store. This was the actual name of the store. It was perhaps the size of a studio apartment, and it was located on NE 87th and 8th. It was the only store I knew of that sold penny candy. When I was a kid, it was electrifying to go in there with a handful of pennies. On this particular day, our objective was ice cream. After peddling all the way there, the ice cream was extremely refreshing. It was revitalizing to stand there eating an ice cream bar with my mom. It was nice to be with her away from the presence of my other siblings. It was rare for any of us to get one-on-one time with her or my dad. After devouring the ice cream bar, she gave me a huge smile. We had trekked the hard part of the journey. Her smile seemed to say that we had gotten a treat, and it would be all easy sailing from there.

Now that I was back at my mother's apartment, a different person was smiling at me. My mother was now erratic and unpredictable. I could not trust her. She was smiling but she might be planning to desert me later. This realization shook me, but I kept it in abeyance. I wanted to focus on the here and now. I didn't want to think about the past.

"Maybe she won't forsake me," I thought. I would not mind sleeping on the floor. It would be better than a bench and a lot better than the group home.

Throughout the morning, we watched some movies that they had rented from Blockbuster. David popped them in. I reflected on the fact that my mother still rented videos from there. For some reason, this comforted me. It gave me hope. I felt like my mother might still be the loving person she used to be. I had been hurt too badly, though, so I was not too hopeful. I had been damaged. How could I surmount the atrocities that had been inflicted on me? I couldn't, so I remained in a state of wary glee.

My sense of glee did not last for very long, though. For lunch, my mom invited everybody out to eat. She said that it was on her. We piled into the purple Cadillac. My mom was driving and my brother rode shotgun. As soon as the engine kicked on, he started messing with the stereo. He found a CD and popped it in. It was astonishing to see a CD player. Since it was 1993 they had just come out, and most people still had tape players. It must have cost them a fortune. David found a song and let it play. When the bass exploded, I felt like someone was kicking me from behind. I liked it, though. It was cool.

We arrived at our destination: Arby's. This fast-food joint had excellent roast beef sandwiches and curly fries. It was near Northgate Mall. We all jumped out and headed to the entrance. On the way, I gave my big brother a hug from the side, and I told him how much I had missed him. He put his arm around my shoulder and said that he had missed me too. We both looked at each other with cheesy smiles.

Lunch was marvelous. I had a melted cheese and roast beef sandwich, curly fries, and a milk shake. It was sensational. We pulled out of the restaurant parking lot with the bass blaring. None of us could hear over the sound of it. From my mom's point of view, maybe this was a good thing. Not being able to conversate kept us from questioning her destination. Conveniently, Arby's was next to an on-ramp for I-5. She easily slipped onto the freeway and headed eastbound. I yelled for my brother to turn the radio down. He couldn't hear me. It wasn't until I slapped his shoulder that he finally acknowledged me. I signed for him to turn it down. He did. I was very afraid. My mom was taking me back to the group home. My brother asked if this was true. My mom signed back that it was. She said that their one-bedroom apartment was too small. She said that she couldn't afford to raise me, and she didn't want the added responsibility. I tried to argue that I wouldn't be a burden, but she would not give in. David and I could not dissuade her. It was frustrating. Mike did not know sign language so he couldn't join in the discussion. He was not happy about the new development, but he remained quiet.

I had come all of this way. I had submitted to all of those hardships. Most of all, I had tasted freedom. I had achieved independence. I could not submit myself to those abusive staff members any longer, but there was no immediate way to prevent my mom from taking me back. We were going sixty miles per hour. Within a half an hour, we were past downtown. Our next stop would be in Auburn. I debated about jumping out of the car. My hand was on the handle, and I almost did it. Then I thought of a better plan. If I jumped out, I would be a derelict. I would have no money, clothes, or provisions. Instead, I decided to allow her to take me to the group home. I would bow to my mother's wishes, but I would sweetly demand some money. If her past actions were indicators of her future actions, she would feel guilty and give me whatever I asked for. Once I decided on this plan, I set it in motion. I did not cry, plead, or argue. I just quietly signed that I understood her position. I would obey her. I told her that I would need some funds to buy things while I was at the group home. She took the bait.

"No problem," she said, eagerly dipping into her purse to pull out two twenties and a ten.

"Perfect," I thought.

It felt dreadful to arrive at the group home. The place represented such misery and pain. Just seeing it gave me the jitters. After being free from torment, facing this place again was excruciating, but I planned to smile outwardly, bear it, and let everyone believe that I was being submissive. I outwardly accepted their authority over me. When I got the chance, I'd escape again. I would leave this place behind forever. Mike followed my lead. Together, we marched behind my mother to the doors of the group home. A staff member opened it and directed us to follow him. We complied. My mother began writing as soon as she was in the office, telling them she was sorry about my behavior. She said that I should be punished for it. They smiled when they said that they would gladly punish us. A shiver ran through me.

The staff members told us to go to our room for the rest of the night. They told us that we would receive a list of punishments when we got home from school the next day. This made me pause in a good way. We would be going to school in the morning. This would be my chance. As soon as we got to our room, I detailed the plan. We would leave from school in the morning. Like the last time, we would fill our backpacks with necessities. I painted a vivid picture of us overcoming our struggles, beating down fate's door, and prevailing. We would come out the other side, and we would be independent.

My propaganda did not excite Mike. He was unwilling to join in this venture.

"No, I am not going," he said assertively. "I can endure it here. Out there, everything is uncharted and unclear. Who knows what would happen to us? We had a fun adventure, but it's over. At least it is for me."

"Don't say that, man! Think about it? We lasted out there by ourselves. We could make it!" I said.

"Look, I've made my mind up. I'm staying. I won't tell on you if you go, though. And you'll probably be better off without me. There will be one less mouth to feed."

"That's messed up, man. I need you!" I cried.

"If you want to leave so bad," said Mike, "you're going to have to do it on your own."

"I need a partner," I said. "I need someone who can watch my back."

"Well, it isn't going to be me. Sorry. I love you, man, but I did not enjoy our struggle. Being homeless sucks worse than here."

"No, it doesn't. It's way better to be free."

"Maybe to you it is," said Mike.

It was no use. He was set in stone. There was no budging him. I would be embarking on my own. Coming to terms with this frightened me, yet I was at peace with it. Being alone was nothing new. Years ago, on the porch of the foster home, I had accepted the fact that I would have to be alone. It was easy to come to grips with this now, no matter how frightening this realization was. It was easy to acknowledge the lonely road that was ahead of me. To me, this was the only option. I could not bear to be here. I could leave. I would be alone again.

CHAPTER 5

When I left for school the next morning, I was loaded down. I had fresh clothes, stolen food, and money. Sleeping the night before had been difficult. I found myself in a reflective state for the entire night, reflecting on the fact that my mother had forsaken me after hearing about how I had been abused. Her explanation for this, of course, was that she didn't believe me. She thought that I was making it up or embellishing it to get out of going back to the group home. Her skepticism hurt me profoundly. I had not been lying or embellishing. Her distrust was completely unfounded. It stung me that she did not give me the benefit of the doubt. Adding insult to injury, she was wasting the house money. How could she buy a stranger an expensive car and not attend to the needs of her own offspring? She was frittering away her wealth on luxury items like a purple Cadillac with an expensive sound system that she couldn't even hear. Where was the logic? It must have been abandoned just like I had been.

After arriving at school, I went searching for Charlotte. She looked breathtaking. I had missed her. We both rushed to hug each other. We did not kiss, but I wanted to. We talked nonstop, updating each other on the events of the last few days. I told her about the challenges that I faced. It was easy to get lost in her beautiful eyes. She talked me out of leaving immediately. Instead, I decided to go to class until the end of the day and then walk Charlotte home. I had no pressing matters that required me to leave right then, so I acquiesced.

After school, we slowly walked down the streets of Auburn, arriving at her apartment at dusk. The slow walk proved to be restorative, giving me the necessary confidence to face the obstacles that were ahead. Being the kind soul that she was, Charlotte offered to shelter me for the night. I would have to hide and sleep in her closet. This was better than spending the night outdoors, so I took her up on the offer. She snuck me in through her bedroom window. Her father was in the next room, so we were forced to whisper. Overall, it was a delightful experience. The mutual attraction we felt during this clandestine activity ratcheting up the excitement.

When we parted ways in the morning, we embraced each other fervently, holding each other like this was the last time we ever would. We ended our passionate embrace by kissing rapaciously. The kiss jolted my senses pleasantly. It was my first kiss. It was sublime. I will never forget it. It was truly spectacular.

That was the last time I ever saw or talked to Charlotte. Regrettably, our embrace and kiss marked our divergence in life. I still miss her. For unknown reasons, I was propelled to return to Greenwood. There was no shelter for me there and no sanctuary. I would be on my own. My mother had clearly demonstrated her position. She would not offer me any support. Therefore, I would blaze my path on my own terms, and no outside influence would impact my decisions. Although I had no reason to return to Seattle, I nonetheless felt drawn back. My childhood neighborhood offered me the illusion of safety. Neither Auburn nor any other city could provide me that illusion. My soul was tethered to my old home and neighborhood, and nothing could change that. The bus ride to Seattle was uneventful. I used the time to think about my immediate concern: shelter. I figured the newspaper bin would be the best prospect. The thought of sleeping on that bench at Sandel Park was not enticing. I even figured out how to keep warm in the bin. I would stop at Thriftko, which was on 85th behind the McDonald's, and buy a used sleeping bag.

When I finally arrived at Thriftko, it was noon. I went in and tried to locate an acceptable sleeping bag. I found a nice one, but it was pricey. It was ten dollars, which was 20 percent of my fifty dollars. I also found some warm gloves and a stocking cap. Furtively, I looked around to see if any store employees were watching me. When I knew that they weren't looking, I peeled the price tag off of an item that cost one dollar. I then scraped off the price tag for the sleeping bag and replaced it with the cheaper tag. Bringing the items up to the counter, my total came to two dollars. I had saved nine dollars. It might have been a shady move, but I had to do whatever I could to save and conserve money.

On my first night alone in the bin, I felt extremely skittish. I had covered the slots with the garbage bags again and unrolled my sleeping bag on top of the pile of newspapers. Using my backpack as a pillow, I settled in. As I was dozing, a group of people walked by. I followed every step in my mind, trying to be alert in case they descended on my shelter. When their footsteps faded, I was able to sleep.

Two weeks went by painfully slow as I acclimated to my homelessness. The initial enthusiasm had worn off by the fourth night. The bitterly cold nights impelled me to seek a warmer solution. No solution became readily apparent, so I was forced to suffer through the frigidity. During those two weeks, I had run into other street kids. They were not necessarily homeless, but they roamed the streets at all hours. I had known some of them from when my old house had been the hangout. One kid in particular, Bobby, was about the same age as me. We clicked immediately. He lived in a big rundown house on 8th Avenue. His parents did not mind if he ran around the streets, so we routinely hung out together. His stepfather and mother were Steve and Lynn. They were liberal parents who allowed Bobby the freedom to find his own path in life. Thankfully, his path coincided with mine, and we become friends really quickly. Occasionally, he would allow me to crash at his house. Bobby first introduced me to marijuana and drinking. Of course, I had been exposed to them during my brief stint in the deteriorated environment of my old house, but I had abstained from consuming them then. Regrettably, my mother's cavalier attitude toward these intoxicants lowered my resistance to them. I had no one to warn me of the grave consequences associated with using these drugs. Most notably, I didn't know that gateway drugs would lower my ability to resist more potent drugs. I wish I would have known this. I believe that I would have heeded those warnings. It is disheartening to think that nobody warned me.

I wandered the streets of Seattle with Bobby. We were often under the influence of marijuana, which had become my drug of choice because it was easier for me to get. Unlike alcohol, we did not need to be twenty-one years old to buy it. And for me, marijuana provided a getaway. I could escape into an alternate world, where I did not need to worry about my physical needs. I was able to ignore my abandonment issues and the physical and sexual abuse I had gone through. I was also able to ignore my most immediate concern: homelessness. It was a welcome experience at the time. I had so much emotional pain bottled up that I was easy prey for the grand appeal of drug usage. Do I regret my past use of drugs? Yes. Would I change this? I honestly don't know. My past is what made me, so it is hard to justify any changes other than the sexual abuse. We are all the embodiments of our own experiences. Lessening those experiences so that they become interchangeable components would murk my future personality and I don't think that's right. However, on a theoretical basis, if given the chance, I would undoubtedly choose to refrain from all drug use. The toll on me was too great. It was too invasive and all-encompassing.

Sauntering down the streets with Bobby became my routine. Under his tutelage I was inaugurated into the School of Hard Knocks. We spent the days carousing and toughening up. Before my homeless days, I had been reluctant to resort to fighting. The constant turmoil of being homeless, though, quickly whittled my reluctance away. It seemed like the streets had their own code of ethics regarding how you should act or react to certain situations or slights. The streets dictated toughness. You had to be prepared for anything. It was abhorrent and unacceptable to allow someone to slight you, so I tried to master the requirements of the street. It was not easy. I was not an instant success. I did not have a naturally hard personality. I would naturally avoid conflict, fights, or violence. For a long time, I could not measure up. I would back out of fights, try to resolve conflicts, and dodge violent clashes. Mainly, I would act tough. I would act like I was eager to fight, argue, or commit a violent act, when in reality I was frightened. When I could not bluff my way out of an altercation, I would get beaten up. This happened the majority of the time, but those losing matches in my teenage years were what toughened me up. That was what the streets demanded.

On one particular day, Bobby and I were strolling up Holman Road, which was a busy thoroughfare, and we ran across a guy Bobby knew. When we approached him, I noticed that he was around our age. It was immediately apparent that Bobby did not like him. Bobby got right in his face.

"What are you looking at?" Bobby said with a mean scowl on his face. "Do you have a problem or something?"

"No, man. I don't have any problem," the guy said, smiling

condescendingly.

"Then why are you staring me down?" Bobby challenged.

"I wasn't. I was just glancing around," the guy said in a provoking manner.

"If you don't have a problem, then show me some monetary amends," Bobby stated as he put his hand in the guy's pocket and took a few dollar bills. "This will do. Thanks."

The unknown person's name was Hutch. I know this because he immediately went and filed a police report for robbery. Bobby and I did not understand the seriousness of this action. Bobby's beef with Hutch went back to middle school. I had nothing to do with their past issues or the strong-arm robbery, but I was present and I had not prevented it. So, I was deemed a codefendant.

Normal upstanding citizens would have told the police the truth. They would have said that they had not been willing participants of the robbery. They would have said that they were just bystanders. When I was arrested for robbery, though, I failed to do this. The street's venerated code of ethics prevented me from snitching, so I remained silent. The police took my silence as a sign of guilt and participation, and they filed charges accordingly.

I was taken to downtown Seattle to the King County Juvenile Detention Center, where I was educated further on being tough. There was no way around this crash course. The juvenile, which is slang for detention center, itself had been built in a sturdy fashion. It was a one-story building that was about the size of a football field. On one side, there were three transparent pods enclosed by plexiglass material. Organized in regular intervals, each pod held approximately twenty juveniles. In all, there were approximately ten pods. The first eight pods were for males. The last two were for females. The two rarely intermingled. While walking past the female pod, you could occasionally gesture or wave, but that was the extent of it. Past the dormitory pods were the library, the education department, and the gym. The pods also shared an outside circular yard that was completely enclosed within the building. Two pods shared each of the five yards. Nothing covered the open sky in the yard, but loops of razor wire surrounded the perimeter, preventing juveniles from climbing up onto the roof and escaping.

The juvenile was filled mainly with minorities. As a white kid, this meant that I was now the minority. The blacks, Asians, and Hispanics were the ruling class. Whites were targets. Preferential seating at the dinner table or television went to the tough gangsters. I mainly stayed by myself. Because of my relatively young age, I was picked on, made fun of, and assaulted. In one bothersome instance, I was caught completely unaware. I was participating in programming, which at this particular moment was stress/anger management, a class they routinely put kids through. A black kid from my pod had decided that he did not like me. He had received an adverse ruling in the courtroom that day. He waited until we were in the programming department. The programming department consisted of approximately six classrooms. Each pod occupied one classroom, but all of the classrooms were transparent. A fight in one pod became a stage performance for the rest of the pods. I was sitting in a desk and chair combination. The right side of the desk was enclosed, so the left side was my only exit. My assailant, who was clearly three years older than me, came up to me on my left side and blocked me in. He did not say a word. There was no warning whatsoever. He just mercilessly rained a barrage of hard punches down on me. They were crushing blows. One of them broke my nose. Another one split my lip. The punches seemed endless, bombarding me until an officer finally broke it up. After it was over, my face was unrecognizable. Both of my eyes were black and blue. My lips were swollen and my nose was crooked. What I recall the most, though, was my sense of dejection. When it was over, I was sitting in a chair and waiting for the nurse. Tears were streaming down my face. The utterly unprovoked violence had stunned me, and I felt very alone and dejected. I was a child. All I wanted to do was crawl into my mother's arms, but I couldn't do this. That hurt me just as much as the punches had. It was painful to know that I could not turn to anyone who cared about me.

The court had given me a sentence of eight to twelve weeks. In all, I spent two weeks in the juvenile detention center, and I was scheduled to spend the remaining weeks at a juvenile institution. Maple Lane was a sprawling complex that was surrounded by tall fences and razor wire. There were approximately ten so-called cottages, and each cottage had a name. Mine was called Pine. Some of the others were named Spruce, Poplar, and Birch. Maple Lane was located in Centralia, which was a two-hour drive away from Seattle. I saw some of the most vicious fights I had ever seen there. The atmosphere was vehemently charged. Fighting was commonplace. The cottages were designed so that two combatants could fight uninterrupted for a considerable amount of time. This was because the communal bathrooms and individual cells were so far from the staff offices. They usually occurred in the bathroom or in the cells. Some fights occasionally occurred elsewhere, such as the school building, the medical building, or one of the breezeways.

One brutal fight occurred in plain sight in the television room. It was between a Hilltop Crips member and a Norteno. These two gangs were bitter rivals, and they were obligated to fight whenever they saw each other. The member of the Hilltop Crips did not see it coming. The Norteno punched him with a glancing blow while he was watching TV. Both of them were older than me. They were probably about seventeen years old. Even though the Norteno had the drop on him, the member of the Hilltop Crips stood up and exchanged blows. They battled for what seemed like hours. In reality it was probably a ten-minute fight, but ten minutes of hand-to-hand combat was a lot. Blood covered the whole room.

They wrestled, jostled, and threw blows nonstop. Afterward, you could not step one foot into that room without touching blood.

Another memorable match occurred in a cell. Out of curiosity, I watched it through the sliver of glass in the door. The winner of the match pounded the other guy violently, but that's not what made it memorable. What made it memorable was what we found after the fight was over. The loser had crapped his pants. During the fight, the feces ran down his leg and spread across the cell. The cell smelled awful afterward.

I only had two fights in the institution, and I lost both of them. One was over a seat that I had sat in. Supposedly, I was sitting in someone else's chair in the TV room. I wasn't. Nobody else had occupied the chair before me. This guy was just testing me to see if I would back down and give him whatever he asked for. I couldn't do that. No matter how much I wanted to avoid fighting, I could not accept being punked out. If I backed down, the rest of the kids would pick on me and the harassment would become endless. It was better to get beaten up once or twice than get attacked endlessly. We fought in the cottage's communal bathroom. We exchanged a few blows and then he started overpowering me. When it was clear that he had won, he let up. Thankfully, it had not been an excessive beating. We were not caught either. The fight did little to my confidence, but it did prove to the other kids that I was not an easy mark. The second fight happened in my cell. I was roomed up with three other kids. Two of them were black and one of them was Hispanic. The fight started over something extremely gross: emptying out the piss containers. The cells did not have urinals, and we were locked up in them at night. By morning, there would be many two-liter bottles filled with piss. Between the four of us, we took turns emptying them out. It was a nasty detail. Nobody wanted to do it, but the process was bearable as long as everybody took turns. The problem, however, was that one of the black kids tried to shirk his responsibility. He was before me in the rotation, so he'd try to pawn it off on me.

"It's your turn!" I stated rightfully.

"Nope. It's yours. I did it yesterday," he replied dishonestly.

"No. You're lying!" I rebuffed.

"Are you calling me a liar, white boy?" he said intimidatingly.

"If you're saying that you did it yesterday, then yes!" I said, feigning confidence.

"All right! When we cell in tonight, we're fighting!" he stated assuredly.

At first, we exchanged a couple of punches. Then he was the only one throwing the punches. I crawled up into a ball, and he won indisputably. It was an easy feat for him, since he was twice my size. I tried to hold my own, but it was impossible. He was too powerful. I considered the fight a victory even though I had lost. After that fight, he quit trying to pawn stuff off on me. The other kids had seen me stand up to this imposing character, so I had gained some respect from the altercation. I didn't get messed with as much after that.

The black guy's name was Peanut. We became friends after things had calmed down. As a matter of fact, he gave me my first tattoos. He did it with a single needle and black shoe polish, tattooing my initials, a cross, and the three dots on my left arm. There was no motor. The process consisted of sticking and poking. The initials created some controversy later for me. I had been writing to a girl who had the same initials as me, and I had told her that her initials were on my arm. She gossiped around Greenwood about this, and my old friends across the neighborhood ribbed me about this. The cross signified my faith. I believed in Jesus, even though I was a sinner. Maybe my faith was what brought me to where I am now. I had no problem expressing my faith. The three dots were commonly known amongst the kids to represent, "Mi Vida Loco," which meant my crazy life. Ironically, I got the tattoo when I was only thirteen. I hadn't even lived my life yet. What I had already experienced at that point, though, was crazy enough.

In addition to getting tattooed, I gained knowledge. The institution was a criminal incubator. Kids spent idle time telling grandiose stories about their criminal exploits. I was more innocent when it came to crime. Peel a price tag off and replacing it with a different one was the worst crime I had committed. These kids would glamorize the stories so they were larger than life. They bragged about stolen cars, high-speed chases, bank robberies, and burglaries. These were older kids than me, and I absorbed everything they said, especially when it came to committing crimes to survive. A number of the kids were homeless like me. They explained the various hustles that they employed to stay warm and fed. The stories amazed me. I digested them keenly, storing them in my memory bank in case I ever needed them. Before coming to the institution, I had never considered committing crime as a viable means of survival. When these guys spoke with pride and glamor about it, I was confused.

"Is that an acceptable way to survive?" I asked myself. I couldn't tell. The kids said that there were no rules when survival became the concern. This baffled me. Up until that point, I had never thought of myself as a criminal. These kids were divulging incriminating exploits, though, like I was a part of their secret brotherhood. It was like I was a criminal too. Until then, it had not dawned on me that I was a criminal. I had not committed the robbery, but I had tarnished my record by implicating myself in it. Forever, I would be labeled a criminal. I detested this fact, but what could I do now? There was nothing I could do. It didn't matter if I committed one crime or a million. I would forever be classified a criminal.

Since no guardian came to claim me, I was forced to stay for the full twelve weeks. If only one person had called, I would have gotten out a month earlier, but I had nobody. When you're young, time seems to drag by. Ten weeks felt like ten years. It was terrible, but eventually the time came. When getting released, the usual protocol is that your family picks you up and drives you to the probation office. In my case, this was not an option. Instead, they transported me in a Suburban that had been retrofitted with a police cage in the back. Even though I was getting released, they shackled my legs and my arms. It was for their safety, they said, but it made the trip extremely uncomfortable for me. I was more concerned, though, about where I was going to go. Where would I sleep, eat, or shower?

I was driven to the probation officer's bureau in downtown Seattle. My probation officer's name was Tony Ginns. He was an elderly guy who was about fifty years old or so. He was cordial, but he had an air of urgency about him. It was like he was always on the move or possibly late for a deadline. There was not much he could do with me. I had no phone, no guardians, no stable address, and no means of generating income to commute to his office every week. I was an unworkable case for him. Now that I was considered a criminal, they did not even entertain the idea of putting me back into the foster care system. In my eyes this was a good thing, but to them it was complicated. They gave me no money and no food stamps. They only gave me four bus passes. So, I went back to where I felt safe: Greenwood. Shortly thereafter, Mr. Ginns filed a bench warrant against me for failing to report. Within two weeks, I was a fugitive.

CHAPTER 6

I t was a relief to leave Maple Lane. While I was there, I wasn't dwelling on the streets. I missed being free and seeing the people I wanted to see. In the institution, my main concern had been about survival. I had had no energy to think about anything else. Now that I was free, though, I felt exhilarated. Taking the metro bus from downtown Seattle to Greenwood, I felt like a new person. For some reason, my brief stint in detention had made me feel more empowered. I felt like I was a man now. I had been to a rough institution and survived, and the staff members in the institution had not mistreated me. By treating me like an independent person, they had unknowingly built up my confidence.

Arriving at 85th and Aurora, I felt a rush of positive feelings. Even though I had no home and nowhere to seek shelter, I felt welcome. I felt like this was where I belonged. On my first night back in the neighborhood, I went in search of shelter. It was not easy to find. I didn't have a dime to bribe a friend to sleep on his floor. I had no incentives to persuade anybody to help me out, but I noticed a difference in my interactions with the street kids I knew. They were in awe about how I had survived the juvenile detention center relatively intact. They asked me questions about my experiences. They asked about my fights and struggles. I had been elevated in their eyes. I was now tougher and more seasoned. I liked the attention. They no longer viewed me as a piece of garbage. I was now somebody who had been through the system and come out the other side.

The celebration among our core group of street kids went well throughout the night. Ton, Ike, Jerry, Red, Little G, and I walked around aimlessly. Ike, Jerry, Red, and Little G were drinking forty-ounce bottles of Old English from paper bags. I would take a swig here and there, but my intoxicant of choice was marijuana. Ton smoked a bowl of weed with me. Ton was older than me by five years. He had been around the block. Some viewed him as a bully, and he had a reputation as a fighter. He'd go around the neighborhood looking to get into trouble. On one occasion, I was walking down the street with him and he pulled out a knife. He always carried one. For no reason, he started popping car tires as we walked all the way from Sandel Park to Safeway.

I was stoned but I remember thinking, "What's the point of this?" I didn't say it to him, of course. I was a pipsqueak compared to him. He performed random acts like this to build up his cred and his persona as being a tough guy. At the time, I thought it was cool, but I don't think so anymore. Now, I think he was a weak imposter. It took me many years to figure that out. I was misguided and lost. I had to settle for looking up to misfits and losers. At the time, I was just glad to have friends who accepted me and welcomed my presence. The abandonment and abuse that I had experienced had tainted my perceptions. I had to take the friends I could get.

I considered Ton a street kid, but he wasn't. He had a home, a family, two parents who loved him, and three younger siblings who looked up to him. His parents were Jayce and Marci. Jayce was a construction worker, and Marci was a hairdresser. In order of age, his siblings were Alisha, Maria, and Ryan. Maria was my age and she was very hot. I was attracted to her from the first time I met her. Alisha was older than me by a couple of years, but she was good-looking as well. As the youngest child, Ryan was kept at home and sheltered.

I don't know what caused Ton to go wayward when he had a family and a home like that. If I had been in his situation, I wouldn't have taken it for granted. I would have treasured a situation like that and used it to be all that I could be.

All of the other guys had homes too. They had places to go to sleep. They had warm places to kick their shoes off, but they chose to run around the streets. They chose to take their families and homes for granted. I did not judge them for it. Like I said before, I was just grateful to have friends I could hang out with. None of them went to school. All of them were older than me. The only kid who was my age was Bobby, and he got sent to Echo Glen, a juvenile co-ed institution. Since his parents vouched for him, the courts allowed him to stay out of the county juvenile detention center until he went to Echo Glen. It was a posh institution compared to Maple Lane.

On my first night out, Jerry let me sleep on his floor. Jerry's parents were liberal. They smoked marijuana, and they did not care if Jerry had friends over occasionally. Their house was literally feet away from my old home. Their house was on Third Street. If you walked out their back door, across an alley, through a yard, and across the street, you'd be at my old home; it was that close, and I liked how close it was.

It was September of 1994. The weather was getting colder. The rain was starting to come down more heavily. It was typical Seattle weather, and rainy days were the norm. This was terrible if you were homeless. After my first night outside, I tried to wiggle my way into places to sleep. Ike let me sleep at his house one night. The next night, I talked Jerry into letting me use his tent in his backyard. I slept in that for the next couple of weeks. He let me use a sleeping bag and a pillow. It was better than having nothing, but not by much. I remained cold every night, shivering like an Eskimo.

While he allowed me to use his tent and premises, which did not include his restroom, his family did not invite me in to eat with them. I played it off like it was no big deal, but it was hard to watch Jerry wolf down homemade meals while I was starving. I'd gather apples, pears, plums, or blackberries to tide me over. At night, I'd beg McDonald's employees to give me their leftovers. Sometimes, they had food for me; sometimes, they had no food. It was a constant struggle to find something to eat.

During the day I'd panhandle, asking humbly for coins. I would typically get no more than a couple dollars. There was no rhyme or reason to my wanderings. I'd transverse the busy pedestrian walkways, looking to catch someone's eye so that I could ask them for spare change.

As the month of September was coming to a close, I found myself exasperated. Each day was a tireless expedition to find food. I longed for the days when adults would provide for me, protect me, and love me. The lonely moments would exacerbate my troubles. The other street kids had homes and lives, so I was frequently alone. The loneliness was almost as painful as my empty stomach. There was no way to extinguish my loneliness. Although a million street kids surrounded me, I wanted to be with my family. My acquaintances lessened my sense of loneliness, but they could not extinguish it.

When I was in the juvenile detention center, I had lost all of my clothes and hygiene products. I panhandled to replenish them whenever I could. First, I bought a toothbrush. When I would use the bathroom at my friends' houses, I would steal some of their toothpaste. I would buy clothes at thrift stores. I occasionally found donated clothing that had been left outside of the thrift store. I would go through these clothes. Most of the time nothing fit me, but occasionally something would fit. I carried everything in a plastic sack and I left things in the tent. If I needed to wash any clothes, I'd take them with me when I showered. I would sneak in to use the shower room at Ballard Public Pool, or I would use the shower at a friend's place. While I was in the shower, I'd wash the clothes by hand, scrubbing them with a bar of soap. Then I would leave them to dry in a sheltered spot in the open air somewhere.

The human spirit is remarkable. While I was suffering these misfortunes, I was not hateful or angry toward those who had abandoned or abused me. Maybe I should have been angry, but I wasn't. I tried not to think about those people. In fits of depression and loneliness, I might reminisce about my lost family, but that was about it. Maybe that was a defense mechanism. Maybe I was avoiding all thoughts of my family to ward off the paralyzing despair that might have prevented me from surviving. No matter what, I was going to survive. I also found that ingesting alcohol or marijuana kept my troubles at bay. These intoxicants provided me with an immediate escape, although this was clearly the wrong method. I didn't know that then, though. It took years for me to understand the hazards of drugs and alcohol. By then it was too late. At first, I did not pay for the drugs or the alcohol that I consumed. Instead, I'd bum a drag or a sip. I never had the spare money to purchase drugs. Eventually, though, I had to pay for them, and they cost me much more than money.

I considered my neighborhood safe and I was comfortable there because it was familiar. In reality, though, it was plagued with its share of crime, gangs, and violence. No big city in America was immune from these seedy elements, and Seattle was no exception. I was not in a gang, but I had seen their influence. A number of gangs roamed the streets. Some people claimed to be in gangs like the Crips or the Bloods, and some people were in offshoots of these gangs. Some of my acquaintances were either gangsters or wannabes. Ike, Smitty, Bobby, and Ton all fell into the latter category. Even David, my brother, at one time claimed to be a gangster. At that time, I guess it was cool to be in one.

I doubt that any of them claim to be in gangs today, though. The prevalent gang in my neighborhood at that time was the Crips. The Crips wore blue clothing and blue rags to declare their gang affiliation. Their origins were in Los Angeles, and the original members were all African American. Nobody knows what propelled a bunch of white kids in the suburbs of Seattle to join the gang, but their African American counterparts in Los Angeles did not authorize or accept them into the Crips.

This rejection did not deter any of them, though. More confusingly, they claimed to a set. A set is an identifiable territory, group, or cause. Typically, the set refers to the original gang. For instance, the self-described gangsters in my neighborhood claimed to be the 74 Hoover Crips. The set, 74 Hoover, got its name from a street and territory in Los Angeles. Ironically, they were claiming to represent a gang that did not accept them. Furthermore, they claimed to represent a specific set that would quite possibly assault them if they showed their white faces in Los Angeles. It was beyond ridiculous.

What was not amusing, however, was the violence. In a vain attempt to build up gangster street cred, rivals would perpetuate heinous acts against each other and each other's property. These were not minor acts either. The most common act was jumping people. Simply walking down the block could prove catastrophic. All of my acquaintances had harrowing experiences. David, my brother, was sitting at a bus stop in front of Safeway when he got jumped. The act of getting jumped usually entailed multiple attackers assaulting one individual. Where the honor or prestige was is in that I don't know. Gangs operate on a different frequency than other people. The second most prevalent acts were drive-by shootings. The gangs would target known gangsters, their homes, or their cars. One of the most infamous examples was the accidental shooting of a female student at Ballard High School. The perpetrators were targeting a gangster, but instead they shot and killed an innocent girl. That shooting made it onto the news, but most cases went unreported. Gangsters would frequently vandalize the cars of other known gangsters. This included the cars of their family members. The Crown Victoria that Bobby's parents owned, for example, was destroyed. Someone bashed the windows out and planted a stick of dynamite inside it. The explosion tore the interior apart. The rivals of my intimates were the Native Son Blood, or the NSB. I am uncertain about their origins, but I am very familiar with their hostility. I was guilty by association. My brother and my acquaintances were known rivals, so I was judged complicit in their ongoing gang war against the NSB's. This added another layer to my continually growing troubles. I had just finished soliciting McDonald's employees for leftovers. I was in a somber mood. The night manager was growing weary of my plight. My overtures were wearing thin.

The night manager had rebuffed my humble request for food for the second night in a row. He had given no reason, but the message was clear. I would get no more leftovers. This made me feel incredibly sad. The sole bright side to my search for food had vanished. Needless to say, the development cast a dark cloud over my world. I searched my mind futilely for a different option, but there was nothing I could do. I was starving. With my head down, I managed to trudge down a dark, deserted street. Night had fallen long ago. The pedestrians were sparse, but my growling stomach forced me to keep searching for food. Then I saw the Safeway.

I entered the Safeway nervously. The bright interior of this twenty-four-hour grocery store would have been welcoming in any other situation, but at this moment the lights seemed to highlight my ragged clothes, my scrawny body, my penniless pockets, and my guilty mind. It felt like everyone was watching me, but in reality they were just shopping, stocking shelves, or manning cash registers. I grabbed a basket nonchalantly and walked dutifully down the aisle, stopping periodically to feign interest in a particular item. Occasionally, I would select an item to put in the basket. I picked up a loaf of bread, some cheese, some lunch meat, some cupcakes, some candy, and a carton of milk. In a moment of wistful abandon, I grabbed an expensive birthday cake. My fourteenth birthday was in two days, I reasoned. Carefully, I glanced around the store in search of suspicious store clerks. Seeing none, I hurriedly marched out of the automated glass doors with the basket and the goods. Once I was outside, I ran swiftly to the dark shadows of the neighborhood, repeatedly looking back for any possible pursuers. Thankfully, though, nobody had seen me.

Elated, I walked with purpose to a remote area to devour my plundered meal. I had not eaten in two full days, and my desperation had forced me to steal. I was not proud of myself, but I felt ecstatic about having food. The food would surely feed me for a couple days if I ate it sparingly. The satisfaction of knowing that I wouldn't need to struggle for food the next day was delightful. Unable to restrain myself, I eagerly prepared my sandwich. The first bite was magical. The second bite was incredible. Not stopping to breathe, I devoured it eagerly. Bits of cheese, ham, and bread stuck to my lips, my dirty fingers, and my clothes as I disregarded etiquette and shoved the food down my gullet. As soon as I had consumed the first sandwich, I made another. I managed to taste and slowly savor the second sandwich. I sipped some milk to dislodge the dry bread. Finally satiated, I grabbed the basket. As I was walking, I picked up a pack of Skittles with one hand and tore the top of it off with my teeth. I lifted the pack into the air and let the delicious candy roll into my mouth.

I become lost in my thoughts. Now that I no longer had to fixate on gathering food, I found myself lost in a memory. I was nine and it was Easter. My parents had woken up early to plant little plastic eggs around the house. Each egg was filled with candy. One special egg had money in it. Usually, David would find this egg, but this year I found it. It had ten dollars in it. At nine years old, I thought that I could buy a car with it. In addition to the special egg, I also gathered a bunch of eggs with candy in them. My siblings and I spent the day bartering our troves of candy. I preferred Starburst, Skittles, and Now and Laters. My siblings, however, liked chocolate candies. David especially liked them. I traded all of my chocolate for Skittles. I took my newly acquired sack of Skittles and watched a movie called *The Goonies*. Happily, I popped Skittles into my mouth throughout the whole film. I started to feel sad as I reflected on this memory. A tear formed and dropped from my eye. I wiped it away with the sleeve of my shirt. I sniffed, and tried to pull myself back together.

Transfixed with my memories and feelings of sadness, I failed to notice the car that went past me. As it cruised past, I heard the music system bumping rap music, but that was all that I noticed. If I had been on alert, I would have foreseen the potential hazard. The car was a red Cadillac. The driver and the occupants were N.S.B. gang members. They had spotted me. They circled back quietly and came up from behind me. When the car came abreast, I heard the doors opening up and people filing out. There were five of them. They were all decked out in red and sporting red rags on their heads. It wasn't until one of them yelled that I finally turned around.

"What's up now, blood?" someone screamed.

As I was backing away, I said, "I don't want no problem, guys."

"Well you got a problem! A big one! You're David's little brother, aren't you?" a guy yelled as the rest of them surrounded me.

"Yes, but I don't bang. I'm not in a gang," I replied adamantly.

"That don't matter. Get him," the tallest one said as they all descended on me.

The first punch made me dizzy. It was a hard blow. I took it straight on the temple. As the second blow came, I charged one of them, punching him as hard as I could. I attempted to burrow through them, but I failed. They closed in on me from all angles. With no mercy, they unleashed their fury. A barrage of punches and kicks toppled me. Instinctively, I curled up into a ball and protected my head. This instinct proved to be insufficient. The group kicked and stomped me out violently. One of them jumped in the air and came down on my head with full force. This crushing maneuver knocked me unconscious. It was the last thing I remembered.

When I woke up, they were gone and I was covered in blood. I had to wipe it out of my eyes so that I could see. I had lumps the size of golf balls on my head. My cheekbone was squishy. There was a puncture wound on my top lip where my teeth had pierced the skin. Thankfully, though, not one of my teeth was missing. My whole body felt like I had spent the night in an industrial dryer on spin cycle. Anytime I moved, a bruised or injured part of my body would scream in protest from the pain. It was agonizing.

Adding to my misery was the food situation. I could not remember dropping the basket. The melee had required me to focus solely on self-preservation. The gang had decided that beating me was not enough, so they had destroyed my food also. They had crushed the bread, the cheese, the meat, and the cereal into the ground. They had completely trampled the cake that I had intended to save for my birthday.

I could not dwell on my lost food, though. I needed to tend to my injuries. Painfully, I pulled myself up. Managing only to stand in a stooped and crouching position, I carefully limped in the direction of the tent. I wishfully thought about how nice it would be to have a home and a guardian who cared enough to tend to me. The few blocks that I traveled felt like miles. The constant throbs throughout my body seemed to worsen as I walked.

Finally, I reached the tent. Inside, I grabbed a towel. Taking it to the water hose, I began to clean myself. Blood flowed and mixed with the water, creating a diluted substance resembling the tropical punch flavor of Kool-Aid. Carefully, I padded my injuries with the towel. Returning to the tent, I fumbled blindly in the dark for toilet paper and some duct tape. Finding them, I temporarily covered my open wounds.

The events of the night had drained me. Crawling into the sleeping bag, I collapsed. Delicately, I searched for an uninjured spot on my head to comfortably lie on. It was easy to succumb to the drowsiness; staying asleep throughout the whole night, however, was impossible. I woke up no fewer than ten times. I kept accidentally putting pressure on my injuries. The immense pain was unbearable.

The next morning, I summoned Jerry and told him what had happened. A long tale was unnecessary; my visible injuries spoke for themselves. Without telling me where he was going, he darted away. Peeking through the windows with my black-and-blue eyes, I saw him on the phone. He wasn't calling the police. Within a couple of hours, Ton, Ike, Lil' G, Smitty, and the others had gathered. The mutual consensus was that we should retaliate. My description of the car gave everyone a clear picture of the driver. Ton and Ike went to Ballard High School with him. Without any further discussion, everyone agreed to wait until dark. In the interim, I managed to properly bathe, swab with disinfectant, and bandage my wounds. Red pulled me aside and we smoked a joint. The high momentarily blunted my pain and it felt great.

When night came, we jumped into three cars. Each car was filled to capacity. Aimlessly, we canvassed the gang's territory, looking down each block and alley for any sign of them. After two hours of fruitlessly searching, we reconvened at Golden Gardens, a park with a beach that served as our command post. Our proposed strategy was to vandalize the gangster's car. Everyone agreed on this course of action, and we formalized a plan. We would park the cars down the street so that any possible witnesses would not get our license numbers. Collectively, we would try to destroy the car.

I felt enraged upon seeing the red Cadillac. The owner and the occupants of that car had brutally assaulted me until I was unconsciousness. Every agonizing step I took reminded me of their callousness. I wanted to get revenge. Retribution is a natural human response. Some people in our civil society think that the courts should be the sole arbitrators of retribution and justice. However, the laws of nature reign supreme on the cold streets. On the street, you trade an eye for an eye.

I threw the first stone. It was a boulder. It went through the windshield. We then threw a barrage of objects, destroying every window. With our knives, we sliced all of the seats to shreds. We battered the dashboard and the stereo. We doused blue paint over the exterior and the interior. We completely demolished the car. I wanted to write my name on it, declaring loudly that I had done it. I wanted to let them know that their heartless beating had precipitated this, but there was no reason to. They would know that I was behind this destruction.

After we were done, we piled back into the cars. The rest of the night went by in a blur. Our sense of camaraderie was clear. I felt inspired by the knowledge that people cared enough about me to band together and fight a common foe. I still held the deep-seated belief that I was worthless. I was insecure about myself in every aspect. The abandonment and the abuse that I had endured had seeped into my psyche. My entire thought process had been tainted so that this exhibition of unity felt extremely uplifting. I understood now why gangs were so enticing.

The next day was my birthday. It was October 2nd and I was fourteen. I received no presents or cake—nothing. I was prepared for the lack of a celebration, but I couldn't help daydreaming about my family hiding in a dark room. I imagined them waiting to spring out and scream, "Happy Birthday." My mother was holding a two-tiered cake with fourteen candles. All of my friends were there. My parents were beaming lovingly. After everyone had wished me well, they presented me with the cake. My attempts to blow the candles out provoked an eruption of laughter. They were trick candles. The more I blew, the more they'd spark back to life. I would laugh right along with them, loving the attention and the sense of acceptance. My parents would each present me with a gift. My dad would give me a new video game; my mom would give me a new remotely controlled airplane. As I would open it, she would proudly state that it was a temporary plane. Eventually, I would get a real plane. I would smile back and tell them all that I loved them dearly. Then my siblings would each give me something. With each gift, they would impart a funny comment. They would each say something jokingly and lovingly. I would then hug and kiss each one of them. I would tell them how much I needed them. I would say that I missed them and loved them. David would put me in a loving headlock and rub my head. There would be so much food, cake, and ice cream that I wouldn't be able to eat anymore.

The thought of food brought me back to reality. I had not eaten much since I had pilfered those sandwiches. Sure, I had eaten some apples and plums, but they were inadequate. I needed something to fill my empty belly. My days of homelessness had acclimated me to hunger. It was common for me to go a full day without food. By the second day, though, my body forcibly urged me to seek nutrients. The urge could not be ignored.

This urge compelled me to go on the hunt. I was in a primal state. My one-track mind smoothly reminding me about how easy it was to steal a meal. I recalled the euphoria that I had felt upon successfully accomplishing the mission. It did not take much mental prodding for me to entertain the idea of stealing again. I did not necessarily relish the act itself, but the ends justified the means in my mind. So, I resolutely headed in the direction of a QFC grocery store.

Upon entering, I confidently picked up a basket and walked

assuredly down the aisle, as if I didn't have a care in the world. I took my time selecting the items. There were many shoppers in the store. I believed that I sufficiently blended in with the commercial atmosphere. I decided to pick out some gourmet products. If I was going to steal, I might as well take the best stuff. Additionally, it was my birthday. Why shouldn't I be allowed a treat? No one else was going to provide it for me.

I succeeded again this time. I pilfered exquisite meats, cheeses, condiments, and baked delicacies, including a beautiful cake. I brought it all to Jerry's house and asked if I could cook it there. This was no problem, he told me. I shared my spoils with him and his parents. The night was topped off with a marijuana cigarette. I smoked it with Jerry and his mom Blain. She had cancer. Life was bearable for her when she used marijuana. At any opportunity, she would blaze a joint. Her painfilled eyes would sparkle alive when the smoke was exhaled. I felt good about sharing her reprieve from the pain. Watching the smoke curl up around her head was delightful. Jerry's dad did not smoke weed. But he was not judgemental about others using it. Maybe at some point in his past he was. Witnessing the agony his wife went through battling cancer may have lowered his resolve. Especially when he saw the visual difference between using and not using. After our smoking session, I returned to the tent, and fell into a deep sleep.

Three days later, I experienced the judicial system again. I had been walking down the street at 85th and Greenwood. It was a dreary afternoon. I was on my way to a friend's house. It was approximately 1:00 p.m. and I was focused on scanning cars as they went by. Ever since I had gotten jumped, I reflexively looked for anyone who might attack me. I did not want to be caught unaware again. I had increased the level of hostility by destroying their car. They would surely like to find me and have a word with me. These words would be choice words, and they would probably be speaking them while they were beating me.

To say the least, my warning system was on high alert. When I first saw the police car go, I did not perceive it as a threat. I was focused on physical threats, rather than threats to my liberty. When the cop pulled over beside me, I began worrying. I did not know that my probation officer had issued a warrant for my arrest, so I walked right up to the cop car. As I was walking alongside, an officer got out. I gingerly tried to stroll by him. He was a tall guy. He was probably six feet and two inches tall, and he looked fit. I would unlikely be able to outrun him, I thought. Then he spoke authoritatively.

"Why aren't you in school?" he asked.

"I was sick," I said quickly.

"What school do you go to?"

"Whitman Middle School," I lied.

"Where did you get those black eyes?"

"I got into a fight."

"Are you a troublemaker?"

"No. We just had a difference of opinion."

"What's your name?"

"Daniel Simms."

"Stay right here as I run your name," he said, walking to the door on the driver's side.

"OK," I replied. While he was busy, I thought about running. I could possibly get away if I jumped over some fences. The thought quickly faded as the officer quickly came out of the car.

"Don't move! Put your hands where I can see them," he demanded.

"All right," I said, pulling my hands out of my pockets and putting them up in the air. "What's the problem?"

"You. There's a warrant for your arrest," he said as he prodded me against the car. "Put your hands on the car and stand for a search."

"There must be a mistake," I said as I complied.

"Yeah, you're a mistake," he stated rudely. "Get your feet

apart and spread your arms out," he demanded, roughly kicking my legs apart.

"Calm down. I'm doing what you are telling me to do," I stated indignantly.

"Don't tell me to calm down! You lied to me," he asserted.

"No I didn't."

"Yes, you did. You said you weren't a troublemaker, but you've got a warrant for robbery," he said smugly. "Now, put your hands behind your back."

"Am I a troublemaker?" I wondered. It was hard to ascertain. I had to acknowledge, however, that I had been veering more toward criminal behavior lately. Shoplifting and vandalism were clearly criminal, but I had committed these crimes under adverse circumstances. I did not believe that I was a bad person or a troublemaker. I was just a struggling kid who had been forced to find my way in the world alone. I had no guidance, no role models, no shelter, and no food. I had not chosen the hand that I had been dealt. I just played it the best that I could. I was bound to make mistakes and break laws. People would view me as a criminal, but I had to survive, even if that meant cutting corners and committing crime.

I was transported back to the King County Juvenile Detention Center. I went through the familiar intake procedures. I stripped down and put on a blue canvas top and bottom. I traded my shoes for tan plastic sandals. They gave me a bedroll and led me down the long hallway. The familiar pods were spaced at regular intervals, and I passed by the basketball courts. Everything was just as it had been when I had left. I did not feel particularly afraid like I had the first time I came here. I did, however, worry about how long I would be forced to stay here.

A guard pulled me out of my cell two days later. I had a court hearing. Silently, I followed the guard down the corridor to an elevator. The elevator took us to the floor that held the different courtrooms. The guard ushered me past the milling public.

People had arrived to offer support and to try to free some of the incarcerated juveniles. The loving parents and siblings reminded me of how much I missed my own family, even though we could hardly be considered a family unit anymore. There was nothing left of my family. It was nothing more than a memory or an idea. We were so fragmented that I had no clue where any of my family members were. If I were injured or killed, there would be no one to claim me. It hurt to think about this.

How had it come to this? I couldn't stop to think about how helpful it would be if I had someone to tell the court that I was not a bad kid. I wanted someone to say that I did not have the money or the resources to make it to the probation office. I wanted someone to say that I was struggling to survive, and hunger and shelter were the immediate concerns that was facing. However, there was no one to defend me. I was alone.

Upon entering the courtroom, I saw the judge and my probation officer, Tony Ginns. I also saw a court reporter and a defense attorney, both of whom I had neither seen nor spoken to before. The hearing started as soon as I was brought in.

"For the record, please state your full name," the judge requested mildly.

"Daniel Simms," I stated.

"You're here today to answer for a violation of your probation. Your initial crime was for robbery. Your violation is for failing to report," the judge read routinely from some unseen document. "How do you plead?"

"Not guilty," I said.

"And why are you not guilty?"

"Before my client answers that, I'd like to confer with him," my defense attorney said.

"Fine," the judge replied.

"Whatever you say can be held against you. My advice is to be silent. Let me speak for you."

"OK. I was just going to say that I didn't report it to the

Probation office because I'm homeless. I did not have the money or transportation to get there".

"That's not a good enough excuse," he stated assuredly.

"But it is the truth," I replied.

"It doesn't matter but I'll argue it for you anyway," he replied haughtily. "My client is not guilty due to homelessness, indigence, and a lack of resources."

"How do you respond to that, Mr. Ginns," the judge inquired.

"I gave the defendant bus tokens to leave and return, your Honor," Mr. Ginns replied.

"What do you say to that?" the defense attorney arrogantly demanded.

"I had to use the last bus token to search for food," I said.

"Sure," he stated dismissively.

"My client was forced to use the bus token to search for food."

"OK, I've heard enough," the judge stated abruptly. "The defendant violated the terms of his probation. He will be remanded to an appropriate juvenile facility for thirty days. Court adjourned."

That was my due process. From there, the guards guided me back to my drab cell. Two days later, they transported me in an unmarked SUV that had been retrofitted with a police security cage that separated the front from the back. I was handcuffed and wearing my street clothes. They took me to Green Hill, the absolute worst institution in the state. It housed the most violent juveniles and it was a maximum-security prison. As soon as I arrived, I was assigned to Poplar Cottage. This was the unit that was on lock-down. After the authorities issued me an orange jumpsuit, an array of poor quality indigent hygiene products, and a towel, they took me to a cell and locked me in. This would be my home for the next thirty days. Three times a week, I got to take a shower. Five times a week, I got to use the phone for an hour. These were the only times I left the cell. My hour on the phone was pointless. I had no one to call. I guess I could have played the lottery with the phone, calling random phone numbers and hoping that someone would answer and accept my call. Instead of doing this, I stayed in my cell and watched paint dry. Every day dragged by. The books that they provided me were missing pages. They contained bodily fluids and gang graffiti. Thankfully, they had issued me a bible. I read it like it was a regular book. It provided a means of passing the time. I did not gather any special insight, religious fervor, or guidance from reading the bible, despite praying for this to happen.

It felt like a year had gone by before they finally released me. When I was released, they followed the same protocol that they had used the previous time. The suburban picked me up and drove me to my probation officer's downtown office. He told me to report back to his office the next week. He gave me a couple bus tokens and sent me away.

There were no rehabilitative programs while I was incarcerated. I received no education and no job training. My probation officer did not offer me any resources, leads on prospective shelters, food stamps, or potential jobs. Essentially, I was released with nothing but the shirt on my back.

Needless to say, the same outcome resulted. The authorities issued a warrant for me. I failed to report. Two weeks later, I was a fugitive again.

CHAPTER 7

Necessitas non habet legem is a Latin legal maxim. It means, "Necessity knows no law." This phrase is significant to me. Essentially, it is the bedrock of my life. At the age of thirteen, I did not know what this phrase meant, but it played a crucial part in shaping my future. This phrase conveys the necessity of self-preservation and shelter. It addresses the effects of hunger. My fateful decisions were connected to these factors. Becoming a criminal was not something that was attractive to me. My criminality had resulted solely out of desperation and necessity. I became a criminal very slowly. It began when I changed the price tag of that first sleeping bag. It escalated into shoplifting and retributive vandalism, and it got worse from there. Other contributory factors included alcohol and drug use. Older juvenile offenders glamorized criminal acts, and my peer's condoned criminality.

Nothing was more influential on my criminal life than hunger. Hunger trumped all of my aversions to criminality. When I was desperate to find food, it no longer mattered where the food came from or how I obtained it. Primitively, we are designed this way. Whether we are hunting or gathering, we all have the primal instinct to survive in any way that we can. There is no disputing that criminal acts are ignoble and wrong, but there is also no disputing that in certain circumstances criminal acts are excusable. For instance, it is criminal to break into a house or a dwelling. However, when people are lost in the wilderness and they discover empty hunting cabins, is it criminal for them to seek shelter and safety from the elements? Some might argue that this is a criminal offense. I would propose that these people literally go get lost. I would tell them to go into the wilderness, lose all sense of direction, and then try to refrain from breaking into an empty cabin. Undoubtedly, no one would sacrifice his or her life to avoid becoming a criminal. Anyone would gratefully embrace the proposition of breaking and entering a cabin. This example mirrors my situation. I felt like I had no other options. Clearly, some people would dispute this fact, arguing that I could have gone to the authorities for help. I disagree with that argument. I resorted to the necessity of criminal behavior while I was in the custody of the authorities. My escape from Auburn Group Home was an act of self-preservation. Sure, I could have reported the abuse, but my response was to run away from it. This is not a rare reaction for victims of abuse. Victims who are children usually respond this way. There are countless stories of child-abuse victims remaining silent and evasive about the abuse that they have endured. Often, the abuse does not come to light for many years. That was my situation. This is my confession, even though I am speaking out twenty years after the fact.

As I felt that it was necessary to run away, I also felt that it was necessary to steal. Stealing began as a solution to an immediate concern: hunger. I did not arrive at this solution instantaneously. It only occurred to me after other legal avenues had been ineffective. I became increasingly unsuccessful with panhandling and soliciting for leftovers. Even then, I was reluctant about becoming a criminal. My reluctance slowly evaporated, though, as I grew older. It was the only way I knew how to survive.

The driving force of hunger compelled me to abandon my reservations against criminal acts. Once I had crossed that criminal threshold, I began to find more lucrative ways to profit from criminal behavior. Shoplifting was a simple and effective way to combat hunger, but it did not offer any significant monetary incentives. Regrettable, shoplifting primed me for more remunerative crimes.

When I shoplifted, I thought nothing of my victim, the billion-dollar corporation. Corporations were only abstract concepts. They were devoid of human emotions and feelings. Their sole purpose was to generate profits for their shareholders. That was fine, but when you're struggling to survive, this abstraction loses its meaning. The feeling of starving is tangible; you feel in your gut. Starvation can make people go to extreme measures. This flawed thought process pushed me toward future victims and crimes. No matter the crime, the victim was always abstract. I did not think of them. Instead, I thought about my needs, my concerns, and my wallet. This, of course, was inconsiderate and selfish. However, with no guidance and no way of understanding my victims in human terms, my acts went unchecked. The justice system only pushed me further down this path by not personifying my victims. The justice system is just that: a system. Their objective is to incentivize plea bargaining. When people plead guilty, the court saves money and time. This also saves the offender the indignity of facing his victim. This, I believe, should be mandatory in all cases. The offender should be made to face the victim. Offenders should be made to reimburse them financially or through manual labor. Instead, our legal system incarcerates offenders in distant remote locations, where they avoid being held responsible for their crimes and they are unable to remedy their issues with their victims. This, I think, is unacceptable. Crimes involving property and drugs should be adjudicated and handled exclusively at the municipal level. In this scenario, this kind of offender would not be intermixed with violent offenders or offenders from different cities. This would reduce the overcrowding and provide the city with the energy and labor of local offenders. Currently, the state is the sole beneficiary of prison labor. This is wrong. The city and the victims of crimes are entitled to this labor. How many more prisons will we build? How many more fathers, mothers, sons, daughters, brothers, sisters, and children will we incarcerate before we recognize that we need a better solution? The current systematic incarceration of our American brethren, in my view, is defective. It is on the wrong track. More people are incarcerated in America than China, and China has a lot more people. Matter of fact, China had 1,350,695 billion people in 2012, while America, in contrast, had 313,914,040 million. That's over three times more people. In that same year China had 1,640,000 million of its citizens in jail, prison, or on probation. While America, the land of the free, had 6,977,700 million Americans incarcerated or on probation of some sort. That's crazy. Over six times as many people, with over a third less population. That is eye-popping. It's no wonder there are for-profit prison operators like Correctional Corporation of America trading their stock on the New York Stock Exchange. They are profiting and exploiting the institutionalization of fosterkids and Americans. Mass incarceration is big money and the American people get the blunt end of it. Is this because America is more dangerous and out-of-control than China? I doubt it. More likely, it's because America's mentality toward crime and punishment is flawed. Then again, who am I to discredit this system? My opinion means nothing; I am considered a criminal, and I have been since I was thirteen years old. My perspective, however, could be valuable. Considering the road I have traveled, my outlook is based on experience.

When I was released from Green Hill a flood of conflicting emotions flowed through me, stirring me into a fretful frame of mind. On the one hand, I was cheerful and excited to be out again; on the other hand, it was distressing to be released from total isolation into the bustle of society. In addition, I had the added pressure of having to look for shelter and grub. Obviously, I was glad to be out; however, being out had its own set of worries. I had been locked down in a bleak cell, where I was completely isolated from people. This did not help me reintegrate myself into society. Initially, I felt self-conscious being around so many different people at once. Thankfully, these feelings slowly dissipated as time went on.

It is not hard to guess which direction I headed in. As always, I went straight to Greenwood. It was my safety zone. The first house I hit was Jerry's. I wanted to make sure that my belongings were still there, and I wanted to see if I could continue using their tent. The weather was getting worse in Seattle. The whole month of November brought torrential downpours. I was used to them, though. The rain pleasantly symbolized the fact that I was back on my home turf. I liked that. What I did not like was the temperature. It was dropping really quickly. Winter was coming. Before long, it would be snowing. I was scared of that. This would be the first winter I would spend homeless. I did not know what to expect or how to prepare for it. I would cross that bridge once I got there. For the time being, I was focused on getting to Jerry's. Once I got to his block, I ran to his door. Smiling, I knocked on his door.

"Hey, Jerry!" I said when he opened the door.

"Wow. I didn't expect to see you," he said with a dour expression. "What's going on? It must be nice to be out."

"Heck, yeah," I said. "I was locked in a cell for the whole month."

"Oh, for real? That must have been a hard time," he said, refusing to maintain eye contact.

"Yeah, it was," I said, wondering why he was acting strangely. "Do you still have all of my stuff?"

"Nope. My parents threw everything in the tent away. Sorry."

"Everything? Even my coat?" I asked, immediately understanding why he couldn't maintain eye contact. "Can I still sleep in the tent?"

"My parents threw away everything, and they don't want anyone sleeping in the tent anymore."

"Are you serious?" I sputtered. "I don't have anywhere else to go."

"Sorry. I wish I could help you. It's out of my hands."

Crestfallen, I turned around and walked back into the rain. I did not say good-bye. I was becoming used to this type of treatment. I just accepted the situation and moved on. There was nothing more that needed to be said. What else could I say? They had essentially discarded everything I owned. To top it off, they had forced me to find a new shelter. It was disheartening. My cheery disposition quickly disappeared. It hurt to think about the coming nightfall. I did not know what I was going to do. I tried not to allow myself to get too discouraged. The trail ahead was going to be hard enough. I didn't want to feel any more negative emotions or vibes. I just wanted to focus on what lay before me. To escape the rain and formulate a plan, I got back on the bus. I rode it until it had reached the end of the line. Once the driver had parked the bus, I tried to stay on for even longer. The driver got up and walked toward me.

"This is the end of the line, kid," he said softly.

"Can I stay on for a little longer to dry off?" I pleaded. "I'm homeless and it's pouring down, sir."

"Aw, kid. You know I'll get into trouble for that," he said, looking into my eyes. As if he felt my pain, he relented. "All right. I'm going to take my half-hour break. Then I'm going to turn around and go back on the same route I came in on. I'll let you stay on until my shift ends. It ends after this route, so you've got to get off before then. OK?"

"Yes, sir," I said, trying to smile.

"Thank you."

"Aw, no problem, kid. I figured it would be nice to have some company while I was on my break. If you don't mind me asking, what's your story? You're pretty young to be homeless."

"It's a long story and we don't have enough time for me to tell it," I said, trying not to revive and relive my sad story. "The short version is that I was put into the foster home system. I couldn't stand to stay there, so I ran away."

"How long have you been on the streets?"

"A few months," I replied, omitting that I had just been released from juvenile detention.

"How old are you?"

"Fourteen."

"At fourteen, I was still at home in New Jersey. We moved the next year. My parents got divorced, and I went to live with my mom. We ended up moving five more times after that. Each time we moved, it was farther away from my dad. I've seen him throughout the years, but we never got close again. What about you? What happened to your parents?"

"They divorced too. My dad is in Tennessee now. I don't know where my mom is," I told him.

"How come you don't go live with him?"

"I don't know. He's got a disability. By the way, what's your name?" I asked.

"My name is Larry. It's nice to meet you," he said, extending his hand.

"Mine is Daniel," I said as I shook his hand.

"I didn't finish my lunch. It's half a sub sandwich. I sure would hate to let it go to waste. Do you want it?"

"Yes, sir," I said.

"Here you go," he said, passing me a brown paper sack that contained the sandwich, a dill pickle, and some chips.

"Thank you very much," I said as I started eating. Who knew when I would be able to eat again? I had to take advantage of any opportunity to eat.

"No big deal. I wasn't going to eat it anyway," he said with a smile. "Hey, Daniel, this route is my route from Monday through Friday. You're welcome stay on my bus for free if you'd like. Just don't tell anybody. If you came on when my shift started, you could sleep on the bus until my shift was over. I'd watch your back while you slept."

"Wow. Thank you, Larry," I said with a genuine smile.

I got off the bus at 85th and 8th. On the different corners there was a car wash, a Texaco, and a mini-mart. It was still raining outside. Dusk was descending. By the time 5:00 p.m. came around, it was pitch dark. Night came early this time of year. I didn't have many options for shelter. I tried to formulate a plan while I was on the bus, but it was impossible. There was nowhere to go. I hated the prospect of sleeping outdoors.

Desultorily, I slogged down 8th Avenue. I aimlessly strolled over toward the house where Bobby's parents lived. Even though Bobby was still in the institution, I thought I'd stop by to see if they knew when he's was going to get out. When I came up to the house, I noticed that Bobby's parents had allowed it to fall into disrepair. The big house had long needed a paint job. The exterior had not been painted in so long that the boards were faded to their natural wood color. Dirt, grime, and sporadic smudges were on the door and the frame. The front lawn was little more than a dirt strip with random patches of grass. Beat-up bikes and toys littered the lawn. It was obvious that their kids had been major contributors to this decay.

This crumbling tenement starkly contrasted its lively, good-natured occupants. Steve and Lynn were both incredibly kind and considerate parents. It was clear that they loved their kids dearly. Not in a million years would they abandon any of their four children. If you were a friend, they'd give you the shirt off of their back. Steve's personality was amiable and welcoming. He was immensely engaging. His favorite thing to do in life was to sit around and socialize. He loved to tell jokes and elaborate stories. He could sit on a couch with a beer and spend all day talking. Lynn would do this too. She possessed all of the qualities of a good mother: abundant love, maternal instincts, compassion, and kindness. The list could go on. Every day, she made a big hearty meal for her family. She would spend hours cooking and never once complain. She just toiled in silence. Her reward was to see her child smile. She radiated unconditional love. The kids were a rambunctious brood. Bobby was the oldest. From the oldest to the youngest, Bobby's siblings were Steven Jr., Ian, and Mikey. They stayed active in sports. They played around the house, and they rode their bikes. They were always up to something. They were all good kids.

I knocked on their mucky door. Steve opened it with a smile and invited me in immediately.

"Daniel, how are you?" Steve said cordially. "I haven't seen you in a while."

"Yeah. I just got out of Green Hill."

"Ah, what did you go in for?"

"Probation violation."

"Daniel, it's so good to see you. Would you like a pop or some cookies?" Lynn said, hugging me.

It was extremely nice to be welcomed into their home. Their hospitality managed to do wonders for my soul. I smiled brightly back at them. I laughed at Steve's jokes and stories, and I learned some disappointing news about Bobby.

"Yep. He's been getting into a lot of trouble and fights, "Lynn said ominously.

"They're talking about sending him to Western State Hospital," Steve said.

"The mental institution?" I asked in disbelief.

"Yes. He is struggling mentally," Lynn said tearfully.

"We think it's because it's the first time he's ever been away from home," Steve said.

"It's hard for him to cope with the institutional setting," Lynn said. "He's a good boy. These are just troubling times for him."

"I didn't expect to hear this. I thought he'd be getting out soon," I stated. "How much more time does he have left?"

"Well, he was originally sentenced to eight to twelve weeks, but he's lost his good time. Now that he's possibly going to Western State, who knows how much time he'll have left," Lynn answered.

"I'm sorry to hear that," I told them. "I'd like to talk to him sometime."

"He calls about five times a week. I'll pass it on that you want to talk to him," Lynn said.

"Thanks," I responded.

We talked well into the night. It had been a long time since any adults had given me this much attention. It delighted me. When Steve got tired, he excused himself and went to bed. He didn't ask me to stay or to leave. I took that as tacit permission to sleep on the couch. I gratefully fell asleep in the thick cushions. I did not care that pop, food, and grime stains were on it. All that mattered was that I had a roof over my head. The squalid surroundings were more agreeable than the rain and the cold outside.

As soon as I woke up in the morning, I made my exit. I did not want to be imposing. It was not clear if I had been invited to stay or not. I did not want to risk being kicked out, so I made a hasty retreat.

The morning air was crisp and fresh. The wind, however, was frigid and cold. I struck out into the chilly morning in search of food, money, or company. I had no idea how to accomplish my aims. That did not matter, though. I was used to that.

When I got to 85th and Holman Road, I spotted a guy I knew. His name was Nathan. He was waiting at a bus stop. He had black hair that was slicked straight back. He projected a cool, suave demeanor. He was known for his scamming. He was always trying to make a buck. We got along for the most part. We were around the same age, so that helped. I could stand him in small doses, but he became bothersome after a while. His problem was that he talked nonstop. That was fine if you didn't spend too much time with him.

"Nathan! What's happening," I said, offering my hand.

"Nothing much. Where have you been? I haven't seen you in a while," he said, slapping my hand.

"I just got out of Green Hill."

"For real. Damn. What was that like?"

"Terrible. I was locked down the whole time."

"That's hard time. I've only been to the juvie. I haven't been to an institution yet."

"Good. You don't want to."

"Yeah, you're probably right."

"So, what are you up to? Are you waiting for the bus?" I asked.

"Yep. I'm taking the bus to downtown Seattle," he said.

"What are you going to do there?" I asked. "Make money," he said.

"How?"

"I'm going to hit parking garage kiosks."

"Oh, I've heard of that. Isn't that done with a metal hanger?" I asked.

"Yep. I'm a pro at it. Do you want to come with me?"

"Sure, but we split everything fifty-fifty."

"Of course."

"All right. Let's do this."

"Did I ever tell you about the time I...?" He started droning on and on about this and that during our entire trip to downtown Seattle. I listened patiently, nodding from time to time and laughing when it was necessary. "This is our stop. Let's go!" he said.

"This is your operation. I'm following you."

"You see that tall garage right there?"

"Yep."

"They charge ten bucks to park there. There aren't any parking attendants either. We'll hit that first one."

"Sounds good."

When we got to the kiosk, I stood at an angle so that I could cover him. He pulled out a bent metal hanger and manipulated it into the slots that people used to pay for their parking spots. Each slot represented a corresponding parking spot. Within minutes, he had plucked five tens. By the time he was done, we had $120 dollars. We split it immediately.

"Wow! Thanks man! You are a pro!" I complimented him. Having money in my pocket again was pleasing. I repeatedly handled it. I was so overjoyed that I could not help fondling it.

"No biggie, bro. We're not done yet. Come on," he said, waving for me to follow him.

"All right," I said, reluctantly stopping to handle the money.

"Here," he said as he turned the corner and strolled up to a parking garage. "You need to stand right here and be very observant. This place has security roving around it."

"OK," I said, nervously scanning the area. There were so many pedestrians, cars, and vendors bustling around that it was hard for me to distinguish between security personnel, police officers, and do-gooders. They all could put a crimp in our action. It was my job to foresee these obstacles. It was what he was paying me to do, and I was going to do it well.

"Hurry up, man. I don't like this spot. There are too many variables," I said, feeling jittery as a crowd of people walked by. If any of them had looked to their left, they would have seen us committing a crime.

"Chill, man. This one is a little harder. Just stay on point," he said, meticulously finagling the makeshift tool.

"I am. The problem is that there are so many people to watch."

Then it happened. A sharply dressed businessman tried to see what we were doing.

"Hey, what the hell are you two doing?" he said as he veered in our direction from the sidewalk.

"Nothing. The darn thing took my money. We're just trying to get it back. It's not going to work anyway. Come on, Nathan," I said nonchalantly in an attempt to fool the guy.

"All right, but I'm going to make a complaint about this darn kiosk. It's a rip-off!" Nathan said, feigning displeasure.

"It looked like you two were trying to steal the money out of it," the guy said.

"Nah, man. We were the ones getting ripped off," I said, slowly walking away from him.

"Damn, that was a close call," Nathan said when we were a block away.

"Yes, it was. Let's stop somewhere to get something to eat. I'm starving. I haven't ate since yesterday evening," I told him.

"Sounds good. There's a seafood joint by Pike Place Market that's got amazing fish and chips."

"No way. Even though it's eleven o'clock, this meal will be my breakfast. I don't want fish for breakfast. How about McDonald's?" I asked, attempting to be frugal.

"Let's play rock-paper-scissors for it," he said, hitting his fist against his palm.

"All right," I said. "That ain't right, man! You're scamming. We're supposed to do this at the same time. You're waiting for me to go before you choose your pick."

"OK. Do it over," he said, as we battled again, "Yes! Fish and chips it is," he yelled triumphantly.

Surprisingly, the seafood platter was exceptionally prepared and served. I had not eaten crab, shrimp, or clams in years. Instead of getting the fish and chips that Nathan had recommended, I picked a seafood platter that came on a large ceramic plate. The matching ceramic dish contained a pool of melted butter for me to dip my seafood in. It was delightful, and exquisite.

"Damn. That was good!" I said, wiping my lips with a napkin.

"I told you. And you wanted to eat at McDonald's," he said, pushing his empty plate away.

"All right. You win. You were right to suggest this place," I said.

"Yep, I'm always right."

"No, you're not," I said, smirking at his audacious claim. "So, where do we go from here?"

"Let's try the same garage we got run off of. There was money that I could have gotten if I had had more time."

"I don't know about that, Nathan. We shouldn't push our luck. That kiosk is out in the open. Anybody walking by can see what we're doing."

"All right. I guess your right. Let's hit some different ones," he said as he got up to go pay the bill.

"Good choice."

We jumped on a bus that was heading toward the Space Needle. In Seattle, they don't charge bus fare if you are downtown, so we would jump on buses even if we were heading only a block away.

"Right here. Let's get off," Nathan said as he got up and walked toward the exit.

"I don't see any parking garages," I said perceptively as I followed him.

"It's not a garage. It's a parking lot. But they got the same type of kiosk."

"Oh, OK."

We found and hit the parking kiosk without a hitch. We didn't get as much money as we had at the first kiosk, but we came close. We grossed ninety dollars, which meant that we each got forty-five dollars. It was beautiful. Since we were very close to the Seattle Center, we agreed that we would splurge. We rode the roller coaster, went up the elevator to the top of the Space Needle, bought cotton candy, and played some carnival games. We both lost at the carnival games, but I managed to have the best time I'd had in years. I spent around thirty dollars. Nathan, however, spent well over sixty. When we were done traversing the amusement park, we went toward a row of vending machines.

"Now what are you doing?" I asked curiously.

"You'll see," he said evasively, rigging a fishing line to catch a crisp ten-dollar bill.

"I think I already know."

"Then tell me, smart guy," he said humorously.

"You're going to use the bill and the fishing line to scam the machines."

"Yep. Have you done it before?"

"Nah," I said. "But I've heard of it."

"I'll show you."

He proceeded to delicately feed a change machine the ten-dollar bill. Once the machine had processed the bill, he'd smoothly tug the bill back out.

"Nice!" I said, amazed.

"Easy as pie," he said, as he was scooping quarters out.

"Does that work at every vending machine," I asked curiously.

"No. It only works at certain ones. Most change machines it doesn't work on. This one is the exception. That's because it's older."

"Oh. How many times can you do it?"

"It varies depending on how much is left in there," he said, stuffing the bill back in for the third time.

"Cool," I said, dumping quarters into my pockets. Some parents with their kids were lining up behind us to get some change, so I nudged Nathan. "Let's go, bro."

"Yep. Let's go," he said nonchalantly.

We hopped on a bus at the corner and took it to Westlake Mall. There was another garage that Nathan wanted to hit. The garage was a six-story concrete high-rise. There were waist-high exterior walls on every floor. A person could lean over the wall and look to the ground on every floor. At some angles, the kiosk was visible from above.

"All right. Go ahead, bro. I'm watching for you," I said, looking up and down the street.

"There is a security crew that roves between this garage and a few other ones, so watch out for them. They have white cars with yellow cop lights on top," he said.

"Cool. I'll be watching for them," I said as he pulled the clothes hanger out and began to work on the kiosk.

Almost immediately, unbeknownst to us, a security guard on the third floor spotted us. He did not yell, wave, or otherwise alarm us. Instead, he quietly called the Seattle Police Department. After calling them, he silently crept down the stairs. Once he was on the ground floor, he began to crab-walk, hiding behind parked cars.

"Damn. This bill doesn't want to come out," Nathan said, jiggling the hanger inside the kiosk.

"Is it stuck?" I asked without looking at him.

"Nope. It's the lip inside the kiosk. It can't get over it."

"Well, take your time and finesse it."

"I will. Just make sure to watch my back."

"I am. Don't even worry," I said. Just then, I noticed a shape moving behind a parked car. "Hold on. I think I seen something!"

"What do you see?" Nathan asked, looking in the direction that I was looking in.

"I don't know. I think someone is behind that car."

"Are you sure? Or are you tripping?"

"No. I definitely saw something move. Come on. Let's move for a second just in case."

"All right," he said, following me across the street. Once we crossed the street, the guard got up from his hiding spot and tried to run us down. "Oh shit," Nathan said as he started running. I followed suit. I was faster than Nathan, so I quickly took the lead.

I ran toward Westlake Mall. All of a sudden, I started seeing cop cars converging on the neighborhood. As I crossed a street, a cop car pulled up right behind me. A car blocked Nathan's path so that he was forced to diverge and run a different route. I did not see him veer off. I was too busy trying to elude the authorities to look back. The cop who pulled up behind me gave chase to Nathan. I ran into the mall. Once I was in the mall, I immediately started to take off my coat. I wanted to change my appearance in any way that I could. Hurriedly, I rushed to the other side of the mall and went out the exit. The quarters in my pocket sounded like jingle bells when I began running again. I spotted a bus that was heading in the opposite direction of the garage. I looked behind to be sure that I did not have a tail. Thankfully, nobody was there. I then hopped on the bus, which took me a mile away. There, I found a bus to take me back to Greenwood.

Once I got back to Greenwood, my heart rate and my adrenaline levels returned to normal. I found myself in a reflective state, recalling the last time I had gone to the Seattle Center and the Space Needle. I had a good time. This distant memory starkly contrasted my recent experience. I could not have been any older than eight years old. My dad's father and mother had come to visit us from Tennessee. It was the first and last time I recalled them visiting Seattle. The importance of their visit was palpable. My parents acted as if royalty were arriving. They cracked the whip on my siblings and me. We had to help clean the house, put the toys away, and fix the yard. The shelves and the refrigerator were also bountifully stocked, which was unusual. My parents rarely kept the kitchen half as full as it was then. My parents would shoe us away from the kitchen so that we would not eat any of the food before my grandparents had arrived; this would have been comical if it had not been so pitiful. The food was such a temptation, but clearly it was just a prop. It was meant to imply a picture of prosperity. They didn't want my grandparents to see anything but an apparently thriving household. How fake is that? *Let's fill the food pantry. Let's clean the house and the yard to impress others. Once they're gone, we can let the food stocks dwindle and allow our kids to starve.* It was ridiculous. When my grandparents came to visit, we went on outings together. One time we went to the Seattle Center and the Space Needle. It had been so long since we had been out as a family that the outings felt festive. My siblings and I were able to enjoy the rides. We went up to the top of the Space Needle and took pictures. We looked through the big binoculars that you had to pay for. We had an expensive meal in the Space Needle's extravagant diner and then went back down. We then took the monorail from the Seattle Center to Westlake Mall. To say the least, it was probably the most exciting day I had ever experienced in Seattle. The outing reflected all of the innocence of childhood, family, togetherness, and love. After barely escaping the police, though, I felt disillusioned. My family had disintegrated. I was homeless and I was becoming a criminal. I had run away from the police for the first time. I felt miserable, tired, and not very optimistic about my future. In Greenwood, I went to Ike's house. I had some money, so I planned to ingratiate myself with him in the hope of gaining a warm floor to sleep on. Ike wasn't there. With no alternate plan, I walked aimlessly around the neighborhood. The walk proved worthwhile. I stumbled on a family that was in the process of moving. They were loading their belongings into a U-Haul trailer. A real estate sign next to a metal mailbox in the front yard indicated that the house was for sale. The soon-to-be vacant home was filled in my memory banks. Maybe I could squat in the empty house if it got too cold out.

I did not know where Nathan lived. I wanted to know whether he had gotten away. Our hectic getaway replayed repeatedly in my head. I was proud of myself for eluding them. In my head, they were the bad guys. They wanted to treat me harshly and incarcerate me. They were the authorities, and I feared all authorities. In every encounter, they treated me badly, whether they were caseworkers for Child Protective Services, staff members at the group home, police officers, juvenile detention guards, my probation officer, the judge, or the defense attorney. They all treated me badly. None of them ever tried to help me. They were either indifferent to my plight or downright rude and dismissive. I often wonder if things might have turned out differently if just one of them had taken even a miniscule interest in me. It would not have been hard or time-consuming for any authority figure to discover what was troubling me and why I was veering off onto the wrong road. None of them helped me, though. They didn't care.

I found out later that Nathan had escaped also. He had run through an office building, jumped on a bus, and returned to Greenwood. I was happy when I heard that. You rarely hear of people evading the police. In all the years that I've watched the TV show *Cops*, I have never seen one person get away. The propaganda machine chooses not to air clips of people successfully evading the police. Instead, they only showed police officers apprehending suspects. It is their prerogative to appear completely successful, but it is interesting to note their blatant bias.

Later that night, I returned to the vacant house. I stealthy crept around the back and peeked in through the windows in search of any sign of life. The house was empty of belongings and of people. This delighted me. It was cold outside, and I did not want to be stuck outdoors. Carefully and quietly, I jiggled every doorknob. I tried to open every window. I was extremely nervous and fretful. This was the first time I had ever tried to break into private property. The cold November night compelled me to find shelter, insistently prodding me with numbingly cold tendrils. I warmed my fingers by breathing into my closed fists. Once my fingers were warm, I tried a window in the bathroom of the home. It was unlocked. Slowly, I opened it fully and then poked my head through.

"Hello. Is anyone in here?" I yelled.

No one responded. I pulled myself up through the window. Quietly, I walked through the house and looked for any inhabitants. There were none. There also were no personal belongings. The house was completely empty.

I chose a small room off on the backside of the house. This room provided the best vantage point. I could hear any noises. I was far enough away from the front door to quietly slip away if someone came into the house. I unlocked the window to ensure that I could escape quickly. Gratefully, the electricity was still working. I didn't turn on any lights, but I promptly turned the heat up full blast in the room that I had chosen. Within minutes, the room was toasty. Smiling, I curled myself into a ball on the carpeted floor and fell asleep quickly.

The vacant house provided the shelter that I needed to survive. The thought that I was committing a crime didn't even compute. I was cold. My fingers were numb, and there was no way I could have survived outdoors. Greed, malice, or hate had not propelled my first experience of breaking and entering. Necessity had motivated me. Did I regret committing this crime? No. How could I regret surviving? I do, however, regret that I had been put in the situation of being homeless in the first place. If I were able to do one thing differently, I would never have been abandoned. That is what I regret the most. I believe wholeheartedly that if my mother had not abandoned me, I never would have committed a single crime.

When I woke up the next morning, I sleepily took a shower, brushed my teeth, and combed my hair. Afterward, I cleaned up every trace of my grooming. I even dried the bathtub with my sweatshirt. I did not want someone to know that I had been there. I was grateful for the warm shelter. I did not want to jeopardize it by alerting anyone. Before leaving, I turned the heat off. Then I pushed the window open, pulled myself up, hopped out, and landed heavily on the ground.

From this vacant house, I left in search of breakfast. With

money still in my pocket from my excursion with Nathan, I bought groceries at Safeway. Entering the grocery store, I thought about my shoplifting experiences. I debated whether I should try it again. It would be easy to do and it would save me precious funds. I quickly dismissed this idea. I did not want to take the added risk when I had money in my pocket.

After eating breakfast, I ambled over to Ton's house. I liked stopping by there. Occasionally, I'd get to see Maria. I had a crush on her big time, but she didn't know this. I concealed it well. She was so clueless of my affections that she tried to hook me up with her girlfriends, Tammie, Nicki, and Melissa. She had introduced me to most of my teenage girlfriends. They were all good-looking. I never had a problem attracting girls. None of them was like Maria, though, so the attraction never lasted.

Looking through the curtains of Ton's house, I saw Maria and waved at her. With my index finger, I gave her the universal sign to come to me. She smiled and came over.

"Hey you," I said, smiling. "How are you doing?"

"Good," she responded. "What are you doing tonight?"

"Um, I'll have to check my calendar," I joked.

"Well, if you're not busy, we're having a sleepover at Nicki's. My friend Tammie is going to be there. I want you to meet her."

"OK. Sounds like fun," I said.

"We are going to put up a tent in Nicki's front yard."

"Wow. That's cool. Do you want me to bring anything?"

"No. Just bring yourself," she said, smiling. "Actually, if you can find a bowl of weed, that would be awesome!"

"No problem," I said confidently. "I'll bring some. What time should I show up?"

"Around 8 p.m. or 9 p.m. Nicki's mom goes to bed early."

"Cool. I'll be there," I said excitedly.

I was at that age when I never could find the right words when I talked to a beautiful girl. I stood in front of her, overly thinking what I was going to say next. I couldn't think of anything to say, so I asked for Ton.

"He's not here," she said.

"Oh, OK. Will you tell him I was looking for him?"

"Yep."

"All right. I guess I'll see you tonight."

"Yeah. And don't be late," she warned, smiling.

"I won't. See you later," I said happily.

I wanted to sit and talk to her for hours. I wanted to ask her about her dreams, her goals, her likes, and her dislikes. I wanted to know everything about her, but I didn't ask her anything. I was extremely insecure. I didn't want to be rejected, so I acted indifferent and disinterested, as if she didn't register as a potential romantic interest.

The day seemed to drag by as I anticipated the coming night. After leaving Maria, I went to Jerry's and bought some marijuana. He gave me a good deal: two grams for fifteen dollars. Normally, it would have cost me twenty or twenty-five dollars. I did not like to spend money on weed, but I wanted to make a good impression with Maria. Luckily, I got a good deal from Jerry. I could easily sell some of it to recoup my expenses. I smoked some pot with Jerry so that he'd allow me to lounge at his house until nightfall. It seemed that I always had to entice or bribe my so-called friends. They never did anything nice for me spontaneously. Maybe this should have alerted me to their potential ruthlessness. I was not presently a rich target. If I had been, though, they would have surely robbed me. I did not want to believe this. I wanted to believe that they were good friends. I thought about our moments of camaraderie. I thought about the time that they had banded and pursued my attackers. I thought about isolated moments of laughter and acceptance. I chose to remember the good times and forget the bad times. I suppressed the fact they didn't really care about me. I forgot about how they had never written to me when I was incarcerated for many days. I did not notice their indifference to my homelessness and my hunger. With friends like these, who needs enemies? They were all enemies.

At about six o'clock in the evening, I began walking toward Nicki's house. I had plenty of time to get there, so I wasted time on Greenwood and 85th. I ran into a short Hispanic guy named Lil' Mikey. I had gone to elementary school with his sister, Michelle. Michelle and I never got along, but Lil' Mikey and I got along wonderfully.

"What's up, Mikey," I said, extending my hand. "What are you up to?"

"Nothing much. I'm waiting to meet Chris," he said, shaking my hand.

Chris was his best friend and Ike's little brother. Chris and Lil' Mikey were both potheads. This gave me an idea.

"I've got some killer buds for sale," I said enticingly.

"Oh yeah? All I've got is ten bucks."

"That's fine," I said. "I'll give you two fat nuggets for that."

"All right," he said as we began walking toward the alley to make the drug deal in privacy.

It's funny. I never thought twice about dealing drugs. I would always do it on a whim, and that was wrong. I should have paid more attention to the consequences of it. If I would have then I could have avoided the pitfalls that eventually befell me. Not just legal pitfalls like incarceration either, but also the dangers of being robbed, beat up, or taken advantage of. On so many levels it was wrong. But it took years of experiences to reach this conclusion. It was not taught as I wish it could have been. Instead I followed examples of others. All of the people I surrounded myself with made it seem like dealing drugs was no big deal. I was only dealing marijuana, but those marijuana deals lowered my resistance to selling harder drugs or larger quantities of marijuana.

"Do you have a baggie?" I asked, pulling out two buds.

"No."

"What about your cigarette pack? Pull the plastic off of it," I said, pointing at his pack.

"Good idea," he said agreeably, pulling the plastic off of the bottom of the cigarette pack.

"Here," I said assuredly, dropping two small nuggets into the plastic wrapping. "Is that good?" I questioned, anticipating that he'd balk at it.

"Come on. Add more than that," he protested.

"All right," I relented. "Here," I said coolly as I added another bud. A good rule of thumb in any drug deal is to give a smaller amount than you're willing to part with. Nine out of ten drug consumers will try to haggle with you, so you give them the smaller amount. When they haggle, you add some more, thereby projecting generosity. This works every time.

"Thanks," he said, smiling.

"It's all good. You're my friend," I told him honestly.

After socializing for a bit, I gave Mikey dabs, a quick slap of the hands and a fist pump, and gingerly walked toward Nicki's house again. I took Greenwood Avenue the whole way. By the time I was within two blocks, it was 7:30 p.m. It was too early, so I decided to waste some time at the Greenwood Library. Recalling the first time I had come here, it immediately saddened me to enter the cozy library. I had been so excited to get my own library card. I was beginning the fourth grade, and my class at Greenwood Elementary had taken a field trip to the library. We walked five blocks on a bright September afternoon. The whole class was giddy and talkative. We were just getting to know each other and discover which kids we got along with. I gravitated toward two kids in particular: a Chinese kid named Tony and a white kid named Matt. We joked and laughed, as if we didn't have a worry in the world. What a happy moment that was. When the class arrived at the library, we all promptly scattered with our respective friends. My three-person crew jaunted over to the sports section. All three of us collected baseball cards. We loved them. Matt and I also collected comic books. Our conversations would revolve between our respective collections of comic books and baseball cards. We would barter and trade with each other. We would provide and receive advice, giving each other tips about up-and-coming baseball players or new comic book releases. My infatuation with baseball cards was funny because I did not enjoy watching baseball games on TV. Sure, I enjoyed going to the King Dome and watching the Mariners play, but that was about it. My dad and David, however, loved watching sports. They particularly loved football, but they'd watch all kinds of sports indiscriminately, depending on the season. Since I did not share their enthusiasm, I did not spend valuable time with my dad. I hated that. I tried to act like I was interested, but they easily saw through my facade. I was jealous of my brother's bond with my dad. They had a connection that I could never obtain. My dad and I did not have a single mutual interest. I would pray that we would find something in common, but this prayer never was answered. Occasionally, I wondered if he would have kept me if I had shared his passions, instead of discarding me like trash. I'll never know, but I still wonder about this.

Wiping a tear off of my cheek, I decided that I could not continue to sit in the quiet library. It began to suffocate me. I could not stop thinking about my past and my family. It was depressing and I had to get out of there quickly. I sauntered across the street to the convenience store. Upon opening the door, I smelled cooked food. The fried chicken was particularly enticing.

"They must bake their own food," I thought.

Looking through the glass of the heated food box, I hungrily eyed some potato wedges and some BBQ chicken. Until entering the convenience store, I had forgotten that I had not eaten since earlier that morning. On some days, I was content to eat only one meal, but today would not be one of those days. Pointing, I directed the merchant toward the potato wedges and the BBQ chicken. I found myself following his every move as he weighed, packaged, and rang up the food. I was hungry. I couldn't take my eyes off of the food. I was like a starving dog anticipating a morsel. Whimsically, I grabbed some pop and gum on my way to the register.

I planned to savor the food and take my time with it. My plan lasted about as long as it took me to find some stairs to sit on outside an apartment complex. Within seconds, I tore all of the packaging off. Dipping a potato wedge into the pile of ketchup, I smiled. "This is good," I thought, tearing some chicken off of a bone with my teeth. Barbecue sauce collected on my lips. After devouring my last piece of chicken, I licked my lips. I then chewed the bone and the marrow into a fine dust and chased it with some fizzy soda. It was spectacular.

My hands, cheeks, and lips had a sticky residue that I had to get off. Silently, I walked onto some property, located the water hose, and turned on the nozzle. After looking around, I swiftly rinsed myself off. Using the inside of my shirt, I dried myself off. Tucking my undershirt underneath my sweatshirt and into my pants, I strolled toward Nicki's house. It was 8:30 p.m. My timing was perfect. I was not too early and not too late. Popping a piece of Spearmint gum into my mouth, I turned the corner of Nicki's block. "I have to have fresh breath," I thought comically.

When Nicki's house and lawn came into view, I immediately noticed the blue tent. It had been built on the grassy front lawn. "They must be cold," I thought. It was freezing out. An orange extension cord stretched from the house to the tent, and they had some type of lighting inside. Moving figures were silhouetted against the tent. Muted voices were steeped in conversation. They were oblivious to my arrival.

In a moment of juvenile abandon, I decided to prank them. Creeping up on them quietly, I padded to the tent and listened patiently to ensure that they had not sensed my presence. Firmly, I grabbed two tent ribs.

"Hey!" I screeched, shaking the tent violently.

"Ah!" yelped the three girls in unison. A head urgently popped out of the tent flap. It was Maria. She looked frightened until she recognized me. Her frightfulness dissipated immediately, and she looked relieved.

"Asshole," she spouted, laughing. "You scared us."

"I'm sorry," I said, placating her as I went to hug her. Playfully, she hit me and then hugged.

"I want you to meet my friend, Tammie," she said happily.

As she was saying this, Tammie emerged. She was gorgeous. She had creamy pale skin, full lips and long flowing brunette hair. Exquisite smatterings of freckles graced her beautiful face. Her body was amazingly picturesque. Her hourglass figure betrayed her true age. She did not look at all like she was fourteen years old. Her full breasts, wide hips, tight back end, and long, seductively shapely legs mesmerized me. My almond-shaped blue eyes locked on hers intimately. I thought that I was in love. She was perfect.

"Hey, Tammie. It's nice to meet you," I said, feeling enthralled.

"It's nice to meet you too, Daniel. Can I get a hug?" she whispered, unable to break eye contact.

"Of course," I said, fumbling as I went to hug her. Electricity bolted straight through me as I hugged her. She fit snugly in my arms like she belonged there. Temporarily, she did belong there.

With this extended and warm hug, she clearly meant to notify me that she was attracted to me. My insecurities were thankfully absent, and I was able to project my confidence and attraction. I did not dwell on my deficiencies. My thrift store clothes did not distract me from my game. My charisma, my swagger, and my handsome face enchanted her. We were mutually enthralled with one another, and our connection was intense. In the tent, we spent the next couple of hours lost in each other's eyes. We could not stop talking, and we wanted to know everything about each other. The other two girls were oblivious to us. It was as if we were the only people there.

"Where do you stay?" she queried.

"Here and there," I said evasively. At first I felt like I couldn't tell her that I was homeless. Then I reasoned that maybe she wouldn't be judgmental or apprehensive. "Honestly, I'm between homes."

"What does that mean?" she questioned innocently.

"Basically, I'm homeless."

"Wow. It must be so hard for you," she cooed compassionately.

"It's no big deal." I replied. I was unprepared for her unabashed kindness and compassion. I wanted nothing more than to hold her, protect her, and kiss her. We naturally moved closer to each other. We were so entranced that we had not noticed that the other two girls had disappeared into the house. They were probably stoned on the weed that I had brought and searching for some munchies.

I tried to remember when I had given the weed to them. I was so entranced by Tammie that I had given it to them absently. I didn't care about it, though, and neither did Tammie. We had not smoked any of it. We were intoxicated enough with each other. We were our own drugs.

At first we shifted imperceptibly closer to each other like icebergs snuggling in the frigid air. Then I encircled my arm around her slim shoulders. She welcomed my embrace and snuggled closer to me. It was amazing. "This beautiful girl likes me," I thought. "Wow! Who else likes me? She must be special." Figuratively and literally, I wanted her. Hesitatingly, I kissed her cheek. She smiled encouragingly, urging me with her eyes to kiss her more intently. I complied willingly. I was putty in her hands. Our first kiss was magical. It felt like fireworks were exploding. We were both powerless to our emotions. We fumbled clumsily at each other, our inexperience failing to deter us. A natural progression followed. Words cannot describe the intense animal connection that we shared. Until the sun came up, we continued our quest to learn more about each other. It was morning when we finally disengaged our arms and legs from each other.

"You are so beautiful," I told her fondly.

"No. It will be beautiful if we stay together," she said.

"You want to be my girlfriend?"

"Obviously, Sherlock."

Smiling, we lost ourselves to another bout of passionate kissing. We couldn't keep our hands off of each other. I had a girlfriend. It was amazing. I loved her immediately. I couldn't believe that such a beautiful person would want me. I didn't ever want to lose her. I began thinking immediately of the things I could do to keep her. I thought that the only way to do this would be to spoil her with material things. I didn't have much to offer her right then, but I was determined to change that.

"This sucks but I've got to go home," she said reluctantly.

"It's all good. We'll see each other soon."

"Yeah. Let's talk on the phone every day. Here's my phone number," she said.

"Sounds like a plan," I replied.

We talked on the phone every day thereafter. Leaving her that first day was hard. I had just met the woman of my dreams. I didn't want to spend one minute without her, but I had to accept it. She had a home and she went to school. She was not willing to jeopardize her life, which was absolutely understandable. I did not want her to lose everything that she had either. I didn't wish my lifestyle on anyone—not even my worst enemy.

In an effort to acquire more money, I expanded my criminal activities. I began to car prowl. Stealing things from parked cars. It was entirely unplanned the first time I did this. I had no experience with car prowling. I just saw an opportunity and felt compelled to take it. There was only one thing that could compel me to commit a new crime: cash. In the ashtray, I spotted some dollar bills and some loose change. It was immensely enticing. Nervously, I circled the car a couple of times. With butterflies in my stomach, I walked down the block to look for any suspicious citizens. The darkened street was quiet. I did, however, see people buzzing around inside their brightly lit houses. The clock had just hit 8:00 p.m. I did not like committing crimes when the chances of getting caught were so high, but the cash was too tempting. I had to risk it.

Cautiously, I scanned the houses in the immediate area. When I was satisfied that nobody was watching me, I tried to open all of the doors. Every one of them was locked. I did not have any tools to use to break in, so I looked for other ways to gain entrance. It would not be easy to break into this new Honda Accord. I noticed a slight crack in the passenger window. Carefully, I reached my finger inside the opening. With all of my weight, I slowly forced the window to open further. When I had opened it enough, I finagled my arm into the gap. Smiling, I unlocked the door. I quickly opened the door and emptied the ashtray. Since I was already in the car, I decided to look for any other things of value. I found a nice backpack, some candy, some gum, and a warm sweatshirt. Swiping it all, I promptly exited the vehicle. I scanned the houses again for any threats. My heart skipped a beat when I saw a man standing on a porch that was two houses down. He could clearly see me. I could hear the throbbing of blood rushing through my ears. The guy did not start running after me, though. He must have not comprehended that I had just committed a crime. He was just smoking a cigarette. Inconspicuously, I sauntered down in the opposite direction of the man. Keeping him in my peripheral vision, I quickly put some distance between us. He did not pursue me. Thank God, he just continued to smoke his cigarette.

I had been staying at the vacant house for over a week. I entered it only at night. I always cleaned up all traces of my presence, and I left early each morning. It was nice to have a warm floor to sleep on, an oven to cook in, and a bathroom to shower in. Every night, I would bring food to cook. It was cheaper that way. Most of the time I would bake a pizza. I loved pizza. I could buy them cheaply, so they were an attractive option.

I knew my stay at this house was coming to an end when I saw the boxes sitting next to the front door. I felt depressed when I saw them. I had not realized how dependent I had become on this empty house. The boxes were probably from the first load of the new tenants.

"What am I going to do now?" I screamed. Hopelessly, I crumbled to the ground. I couldn't help but cry. I felt so defeated and alone. I was trying to find my way, but obstacles kept popping up.

My slow evolution with criminal activity seemed to bolster my prospects of surviving on my own, but I still felt terribly troubled about becoming a criminal. I did not like the direction that my life was going in. I was struggling. I had to find a place to live. Sleeping outdoors was not an option in winter. I'd freeze to death. I had to figure something else out quickly.

The next night, my fears about the house were confirmed. A car was parked in the driveway of the house. Someone had moved in. Staying there was no longer an option.

It was well past midnight when I finally formalized a plan. I decided to spend the night car prowling for the stereo equipment, rather than cash. Of course, I did not plan to turn down cash or valuables if I ran across them.

Along with Brian, Ton had schooled me on how to make money car prowling. He told me what to look for inside the cars, and he also taught me how to steal cars. Brian was my brother's friend, and I also considered him to be my own friend. He was tall. He had black hair and he was one of the first guys I knew who had a car. He was an amateur car flipper. I don't know how he did it, but he managed to have a new car every week. He'd trade them, barter them, sell them, and even steal them. He loved cars. He also loved to steal stereo systems. He'd go car prowling for them and then put them in his many cars. His skills at car prowling were notorious. At one point, he even partnered with

David, and they car prowled together. I would get tips and tidbits of information from them. Whenever we were walking down the street, lounging at Sandel Park, smoking marijuana, or drinking beer, they would brag about how to car prowl or steal a car. I would soak their instructions up like I was sponge.

Instead of engaging in criminal activities, I should have been soaking up education. I should have been studying math, English, and history. I now have an insatiable thirst for education. I love it. I can't get enough of it. I can spend hours reading grammar books, history books, or financial books. I've got subscriptions to all different types of informational magazines. I always have a book in my hand. I feel like I was cheated out of gaining an education when I was younger. I know I would have succeeded in school. I would have graduated from middle school, high school, and then college with flying colors. This fact haunts me and makes me angry. Figuratively and literally, my parents and my abusers destroyed me. They annihilated my future, and I can never experience what might have been. This hurts me immensely.

With all of the knowledge that I had gathered from my various sources, I set off to car prowl. My pockets were bulged with tools: a flashlight, a flathead screwdriver, a Phillips head screwdriver, and wire cutters. My pockets were puffing out tellingly. I was hoping that no police officers would pass me. I tried to stay on the side streets, which were ideal because they were inadequately lit. I would walk down the street and peer into every car with the flashlight. When I discovered a stereo or another item of value, I would set about getting into the car. My method of entry varied from car to car. For instance, in Jettas I would pry my flathead screwdriver between the door handle and the car door. Then I would tool around between them until I found the mechanism that would unlock it. For Honda Accords, I would pry either the driver or passenger window and then forcefully pull it down like I had on my first car prowl. With most other cars I would dig the round metal key port out with the flathead screwdriver. Once it was completely out, I would find the metal prong that controlled the unlocking mechanism. Then I was in; it was that simple. If I were dealing with an especially tough car to break into, I'd settle for my last resort. I would simply break the window. Preferably, I would break a wing window to create less noise. In a crunch, though, any window would work.

It is noteworthy that I never broke into a car or a house with any Christian insignia, and I wouldn't let any of my crime partners do this either. I couldn't bring myself to stoop that low. I carried fond memories of religion. I refused to betray my memories. I would avoid fish bumper stickers, crosses, biblical verses, and Christian religious images like they were kryptonite. I would attempt to break into every car on a block, except for the ones with crosses hanging in the mirrors. Even if valuables were clearly visible, I would avoid these cars. The same was true with all my subsequent crimes. In addition, I have never stolen from a friend or a family member. I could never do that. I have always valued my close relationships like gold. My sense of loyalty and blind trust was not always a good thing, though, particularly with regard to my parents. Eventually, I extended my sense of loyalty to my so-called friends. I refused to steal from religious strangers or family and friends, but this does not excuse my criminal conduct. I didn't know that then, but I do know it now. Now, however, it is way too late.

Shining the light into each car's interior, I finally discovered a nice stereo. It was a Pioneer pullout tape player, and the car was a Camaro. Both of the doors were locked. I chose to work on the passenger-side door lock. From here, the car would block me from passing cars so that I could work uninterrupted. With my flashlight nestled between my teeth, I crouched down and began to dig the lock out. It was a complicated lock. I tried to dig it out like Brian had explained, but the lock refused to come out. After ten minutes, I was sweating but I refused to relent. Finally, I dug it out and unlocked the door.

As soon as the door opened, the dome light came on. Immediately, I disengaged it. I did not feel comfortable getting all the way into the Camaro, so I leaned halfway in and halfway out. Carefully, I went through the back seat, the middle console, and the glove box. I looked under both of the front seats and then in the side door consoles. I found some change, a beanie cap, and some gloves. After I had tucked these items away, I focused on the stereo. I promptly grabbed the pullout, put it in my backpack, and began working on the sleeve. I wedged the flathead screwdriver between the sleeve and the car's interior temperature gauge. Once I had bent the sleeve enough, I began to force down the prongs, which held the stereo in place. Around the sleeve, I needed to bend the prongs. Without bending them, the stereo would never come out. Eventually, I got the sleeve completely out. Then I cut the wires that were connected to it. That was it. I had done the job well.

Throughout the night, I repeated this pattern. In total, I found three more stereos. All of them were pullouts. I also stumbled upon a whole stereo system. It had two ten-inch subwoofers, an amplifier, an equalizer, and some tweeters. I spent over an hour dissembling it all. Sweat was pouring off of me. It was a chore to unscrew all of the tight screws. Wiping the sweat off of my brow, I carefully pulled the speaker box out. Then I crammed the rest of it into my backpack. The backpack was so full that I could not zip it up completely. The flap gaped open, allowing anyone to see the contents. This was not good. I decided I had to stash everything. With my overflowing pockets and backpack, I lifted the heavy box and began to walk down the dark street. After five blocks, I couldn't go any farther. My arms felt like jelly. I settled down in a graveled alley and located some bushes where I could hide everything. It was a good spot; people did not frequently travel along this road.

I felt much better after I had stashed the loot. The weight

was not my only burden. It was stressful to lug stolen goods down the street. Every car that went by was a potential threat. Whenever I saw headlights, I would scurry behind a car, drop the goods, and then walk nonchalantly until the car passed me by. It was a tiring process, but it was mandatory. I did not want to risk being caught with stolen items, so I took this precaution until I was able to hide these goods.

With the easy part of the night behind me, I began to focus on the hard task of stealing a car. I had never done it before, so the pressure was intense. Ton had taught me how to do it, and his abstract lesson was the only help that I would get. I did not have the luxury of further instructions. There were no smartphones back then, so all I had was my memory bank. I only knew how to take vehicles with tilted steering wheels. I had only driven once in my life, so it would be hard to maneuver with such limited knowledge.

That one driving experience was very different from the drive that I was about to experience. My first time driving was in a Chevy citation, which was a cheaper style hatchback. It belonged to Brian. He had pulled up in front of Jerry's house, tossed the keys to me, and asked me to park the car. I gladly complied. He didn't know that I had never driven before. He probably wouldn't have cared, though, since the car was one of many beaters that he would quickly barter off. I didn't care that the car was in bad shape; I hopped into it like it was a Lexus, taking my time to position the seat and the mirror. I turned on the radio and even put my seat belt on. I had to be safe. The car was already in the middle of the street, so I didn't have to navigate around any parked cars. I knew the basics. I knew where the gas pedal, the brake pedal, and the gearshift were. I knew how to use them, but I was a novice. I slowly put the gearshift into drive. With one foot on the gas pedal and the other on the brake, I hesitantly put pressure on the gas pedal. I immediately reacted to the sensation of moving by slamming the brakes on. The car whipsawed to a stop. I repeated this knee-jerk movement until I was confident enough to adequately steer the moving car. It took a minute for me to learn how much to press down on the gas pedal and the brake pedal. Once I learned this, I began to get comfortable behind the wheel. I had the radio up full blast. I was bobbing my head along with the song. Smiling, I came to a complete stop at every corner, looked both ways, and then proceeded.

Looking around for any cars, I remained very vigilant. I went two blocks down and returned to Jerry's street. It seemed like finding parking was harder than driving. It took me a moment to park between two cars, but I managed to do so alone.

It's interesting for me to look back over my life and recall all of my first experiences, most of which I undertook without any guidance. I would have liked to have someone to guide me, but that was not an option. Instead, I had to learn to do things on my own. For instance, I had to learn on my own how to shave. For the longest time, I shaved haphazardly. I would cut myself every time. I didn't know that I was supposed to follow in the direction that my hair grew. My first shaving experience was at the juvenile institution. I didn't even need to shave; I just wanted to experiment. Some of my first experiences were positive and some were negative, but I experienced almost all of them alone.

As soon as I saw the Buick Regal, I knew that it was the one. It was parked in a detached carport that concealed it from passing cars. With my gloves on, I pulled my flathead screwdriver out and cautiously tried to open the door in case it was unlocked. It wasn't. Without preamble, I began prying and digging out the lock on the driver's side. I unlocked it within a minute. Getting into the car, I sunk into the plush seat. It felt immeasurably comfortable, but I could not enjoy the comfort until I was not in danger. The first thing I did was wedge the flathead screwdriver into the neck of the steering wheel. My objective was to pry the casing off of the neck. Once I had accomplished this, I saw the triangle-shaped metal lever that Ton had described. Meticulously,

I maneuvered the lever from its original position, and I pulled it toward me. As soon as I did this, the dash lights came on. I had power. The car's engine would turn over if I continued to pull the lever, but I couldn't do that yet. Ton had said that I would need to break the lock on the steering wheel. If I didn't do this, I would not be able to navigate the car. It would have been unwise to run the engine before I had unlocked the steering wheel. With both feet planted on the door on the driver's side, I gripped the steering wheel with all of my might and pulled it toward me. Reluctantly, the wheel clunked to the right. I repeated this process in the opposite direction. Again, the wheel reluctantly turned to the left. I repeated this process in both directions for as far as the wheel would turn. Eventually, I broke the steering lock and I no longer felt the clicks and kinks of the locking mechanisms when I turned the wheel. I had done it.

I could lie and say that I didn't feel any sense of accomplishment, but that would not be true.

It was harrowing to back out of the carport. I tried to keep the car angled correctly, but it wasn't easy. In my inexperience, I tended to overcompensate one way or the other. I narrowly missed a post and then a metal garbage can. Ultimately, however, I managed to back the car down the driveway and pull it out onto the street. Turning the radio up full blast, I cheerfully sang along with the song. I was beaming. I moved my arms, legs, and head in sync with the rhythm. It was an exhilarating sensation.

I was flushed with relief, joy, and jubilee. Pleasure coursed through me like an intoxicant.

I had not stolen the car for joyrides, though. I planned to use the car in a number of ways, one of which was a shelter. I needed a temporary home to keep the numbingly cold Seattle winter at bay. With the heat blowing on me, I drove to the alley. The stashed goods were where I had left them. I quickly lugged them into the back seat and then jumped back into the warm car. It was around 5:00 a.m. People would start waking up soon, so it was best to call it a night.

I drove to an apartment complex with an underground parking garage and looked for a parking spot in a secluded area. When I found one, I pulled right in. When the neighborhood woke up, people would be reporting the thefts. The cops would be coming. It would be best for me to stay off of the roads until about twelve or one o'clock in the afternoon. By that time, all of the thefts would have been reported and the cops on the morning shift would be clocking out.

I gratefully reclined the plush seat as far back as it would go. Then I nestled into it and pulled my arms inside my shirt. When I found a comfortable position, I settled in for a quick slumber. I fell asleep immediately.

Frequently, when I was in a state of deep sleep I would get nightmares. The nightmares were always the same, and I still get them to this day. Whenever I get them, I wake up in a cold sweat. The dreams always begin with me walking down a dark alley in downtown Seattle. The buildings on both sides of the alley are made of red bricks. There are no windows, but there are a number of doorways. As I walk by the doorways, I can vaguely hear various sounds emanating from them. Each doorway projects different sounds. The sewer drains emit a smoky exhaust that billows up, creating a haunting effect. I am never older than ten years old in these dreams. I am holding a G.I. Joe figurine with both my hands. My arms are clenched fearfully around my chest. There are tears on my cheek, and I am screaming, crying, and pleading for help. The doorways screech at me tauntingly. They are ridiculing me, teasing me, and threatening me. The alley never ends. Rodents scurry between my feet. The overpowering emotion is fright. It is pervasive I can taste it. When I go near a doorway, I sense movement. Because it's too dark, I don't see the movements, but I feel them. Someone is there. I detect an evil and dangerous presence. It shuffles and rustles, as if it is wearing thick garments or robes that drag on the soiled ground.

No matter how hard I try to look, I can't see it. I try to get closer so that I can get a better look. Old, bloody, and shriveled hands then come out of the darkness and grab me. I scream. Panicking, I try to back out of the doorway, but it is futile. He's got me. He's pulling me in. Helplessly, I screech a deathly curdling sound. It sounds like I'm dying. It's horrifying.

This horrendous sound woke me up in the car. I felt startled and disoriented. I was out of breath. Sweat was dripping off of me. I could not shake the fear. I looked around fretfully. Finally, I realized that I was safe. It was just my recurring nightmare, but it took a moment of steady breathing to calm down.

Sufficiently at ease, I looked at my watch. It was three o'clock in the afternoon. I had slept longer than I had meant to, but that was OK. Leaving the car where I had parked it, I ambled to the convenience store across the street. With the change I had found in the other cars, I bought breakfast and lunch. I had bagels with cream cheese and slices of ham. I also had orange juice and powdered donuts. It was the brunch of an outcast.

I opened the carton of orange juice as I was walking to the phone booth. After stopping to take a sip, I finally reached for the phone. Before I dialed, I opened up my packages of food. I wanted to call Tammie.

"Hello," Tammie said in her sweet voice.

"Hey beautiful," I said.

"Hey, baby," she replied.

"How was school?" I asked.

"Oh, it was all right. We had a quiz in one of my classes."

"Is Maria in any classes with you?" I asked.

"Yep. I usually hang out with her during lunch too," she said.

"That's cool. At least you've got a friend to hang with."

"Yeah. What did you do today?"

"Umm, I slept," I said hesitantly. I was unsure about confiding in her about my criminal activity.

"You slept? It's past 3:00 p.m. I hope you're not becoming a bum," she said, laughing.

"I'm not," I replied defensively. I took offense whenever people used that word flippantly. I knew I fit the definition of it, but I struggled to present myself well. I didn't want people to look at me and be able to tell that I was homeless. I especially didn't want Tammie and my other friends to think of me this way. I was a typical teenager; I wanted to impress girls. Every time I went to see Tammie, I would take a shower and put on clean clothes. If I didn't have a place to shower, I'd just go to the Ballard Public Pool.

"Then what did you do last night to make you sleep all day?" she questioned.

"Ah, I walked around," I said vaguely.

"Why?"

"The place I've been crashing at is no longer vacant."

"Daniel, where did you sleep?"

"In a car," I said reluctantly. I didn't want to lie to her, but I knew that she wouldn't be satisfied with this answer. "I borrowed a car from a guy I know."

"Who would loan you a car? You're not even fifteen yet,"

"I know. Let's just say I made him an offer he couldn't refuse."

"Does the car drive well?" she asked.

"Yeah."

"Well, can we hang out? I miss you."

"Um, yes. I would like that. I've got to do some things first, though," I said.

"All right. That's fine. What time will you make it over here by?"

"Around five or six o'clock. Is that cool?" I asked. Tammie lived with her dad in an apartment in Fremont. I liked going to Fremont. It was a quirky community. The people who lived there had alternative mindsets. They sponsored numerous parades, races, and events. Every year, they would have a Fourth of July fireworks display at Gasworks Parks. Gasworks was a big and unique park with a huge covered area that housed huge pipes, gaskets, tubes, and various other metal structures. It was truly a one-of-a-kind place. For one of the races that they held there, hundreds of people rode their bikes naked or partially nude. It was a fun neighborhood, to say the least.

"Hell yeah. That's cool. I can't wait to see you," Tammie said.

"All right babe. See you then. Bye," I said.

"Bye," Tammie said.

After I hung up, I dialed Dave's number. Dave was a friend of my brother, David, and I had become friends with him too. He was my fence. The person that would buy all my stolen car equipment. I knew that I would need one, so I had gotten his number from Ton. Dave was a fair fence. He had numerous sources of revenue, one of which was selling cocaine. This gave him the resources to buy large quantities of stolen goods. He'd buy anything. He stood out in the neighborhood because of his extravagant cars and rims. His hairstyle was also noticeable. He had a mullet. Even in the nineties, that hairstyle was a no-no.

"Hello," Dave answered.

"What's up, Dave? This is Daniel."

"What's happening Daniel? How are you?"

"I'm all right. Are you busy? I've got some merchandise to show you," I said.

"Nope. I'm free. Let's meet at Sandel Park."

"Cool. That'll work. How long from now?" I asked. As I was asking this, I turned around to see a Seattle police officer pulling into the parking lot.

"Be there in twenty minutes. What do you have, by the way?"

"Um." This was all that I could say. The police officer was walking right toward me. Oh no! Should I run? I didn't have time to react.

CHAPTER 8

He descended upon me too quickly. I tried to act nonchalant and unworried about his presence, but I was certain that he would see through my facade. Adrenaline rushed through me. My heart skipped a beat when he was standing right beside me. He was so close that I could hear him breathing. Just as I thought he was going to grab me and put handcuffs on me, he walked right past me. He was going to the convenience store. "Oh, thank God," I thought appreciatively.

I endured many moments like that. Whenever I saw a cop, I got extremely nervous. My palms got sweaty, and my body temperature elevated abnormally. Adrenaline flooded my senses. I believe that I had a primal, fight-or-flight instinct to respond this way. The cops were my predators. Every ounce of my being became very aware when I saw them. If I were to list all of the times that I ran from police officers, this book would be longer than a thousand pages. I kept looking for new routes that would help me elude them. I kept looking for places to hide from them. I had to do this because I knew that they were looking for me.

From the day I got released for being an accomplice to robbery until the present day in 2013, I have not been able to complete my probation. I have perpetually had outstanding warrants, and this is pitiful. I am embarrassed to admit it. In my defense, though, the odds were against me. I was a troubled soul. I didn't have support. I had no guidance, no positive role models, and no assistance. I had nothing. Every time I was released, I had to forge my own path and start from scratch. Since I was kid, it was especially hard.

"I'm sorry. What did you say, Dave?"

"Where did you go?"

"I was here but a cop was walking toward me and I got skittish. Sorry."

"It's all good. I was asking what type of goods you had."

"Oh yeah," I said. "I've got four nice pullouts, an amplifier, some equalizers, some tweeters, and ten-inch speakers."

"Damn. Hell yeah! I want all of it."

"All right. See you at Sandel. Bye," I said, hanging up.

I didn't like the idea of driving a stolen car in broad daylight, but the situation was unavoidable. I had to transport the goods. I couldn't walk the goods to Dave, and I had promised Tammie that I would meet up with her. I couldn't disappoint her; she meant too much to me. Just thinking of her made me smile.

I had to drive the car, but I wasn't going to do it until the cop was long gone. I waited across the street until he got into his car and pulled out. I waited for five minutes to let him get ahead of me, and then I put my gloves on and opened the car door. I didn't want to leave fingerprints. Grabbing the flathead screwdriver, I quickly started the car up. I looked at how much gas I had. I almost had a full tank. Nice.

The radio was playing a Tupac song called "Dear Mama." It made me think about my mom. Where was she? What about David? I heard through the grapevine that they had moved to Edmonds, Washington. They were living close to Stevens

Hospital. I didn't want to allow my mom to possibly send me back to the group home, so I stayed away from them. I still missed them, though.

I saw Dave as soon as I pulled up to Sandel Park. He was in a tan Monte Carlo with golden wire rims. He was clearly flaunting his wealth. I found myself envious. I didn't want his wealth, but I aspired to be like him. I wanted to have a nice car and clothes like he had. I knew that I wouldn't become like him through car prowling and petty theft. I needed a more lucrative operation. I needed something that had the potential to makes lots of money. I thought about dealing drugs. It seemed easy. I could get into the game relatively quickly, but I didn't have a clue about how much to charge, where to get clients, or how to deal with that type of clientele. Cokeheads are a lot different than potheads. Cocaine is addictive, and cokeheads would spend their last dollar on it. Furthermore, cokeheads are unpredictable. You never knew what to expect from them. For the time being, I decided against selling cocaine.

"There you are! I've been here for ten minutes waiting for you," Dave said impatiently.

"Sorry. I was waiting for that cop to get away from me."

"Oh, OK. So, let's see the goods."

"All right," I said, opening the passenger door. "Just so you know, this car is stolen. Don't touch anything."

"Thanks for the warning. I won't touch it. As a matter of fact, let's just bring the goods to my car. We'll look at them there," said Dave.

"OK."

"Damn. This speaker box is heavy," he said as he lugged it to his car.

"Yeah. I carried that sucker for five blocks, along with this full backpack."

"That's impressive," he joked. "You missed your calling. You should be a manual laborer."

"What's wrong with working for a living?" I responded.

"That's lame. There are plenty of ways to make money without having to work for it."

"Yeah. Illegally," I said.

"So? Money is money."

"Whatever. Do you like the merchandise?" I asked as he was examining an Alpine pullout. "I'm going to want top dollar for these babies. They were all in good condition."

"They aren't all that. I'll give you twenty dollars a pullout, so eighty bucks for all of them."

"No way, dude. The pioneer is worth more than that! So is the Alpine! The JVC and Panasonic might go for twenty. But I want forty for the other two I said". Haggling was a way of life. You never got what you asked for unless you sat on it for a long time. There was no eBay back then.

"Nope. I'll give you thirty for those two."

"No way. I might go to thirty-eight."

"Thirty-five."

"Fine. What about the other stuff?"

"I want that too, but let's take a toke of weed first," he said, passing me a metal pipe that was packed with bud.

"Sure," I said, grabbing it.

"For our deal, I'm going to want some weed too. Is that OK?"

"Yep. That's fine. I got plenty."

"Cool," I said, flicking the lighter and lighting the pipe. I took a big toke, choked, and then sputtered the smoke out. It was strong weed. I got high immediately. I passed the pipe to him and he took a toke too. "That's good stuff."

"Yeah. I got it in the U District," he said, exhaling smoothly. "It's U-Dub bud."

"Wow. That's awesome," I said, feeling stoned. The U District is where the University of Washington is located. The marijuana that came from there was notoriously good. They said that it was hydroponic, which meant that they grew it with water but no dirt. They used all kinds of up-to-date agriculture products to ensure its quality.

"All right. I'll give you twenty bucks for the equalizer, fifty for the amplifier, and seventy for the..." He stopped to take a toke. Then he exhaled and said, "Speaker box."

"Um." All of my haggling skills had disappeared. I was stoned but Dave seemed unaffected. "Look, I'm not going to haggle with you. I said. This is my best offer. Add ten dollars on each item and you've got a deal," I said.

"Deal," he said quickly, grabbing my hand to shake it.

"Maybe I should have charged more," I thought slowly. It was too late, though. A deal was a deal.

"So, how much weed and how much cash do you want? Altogether, it comes out to $210."

"Um. How about sixty in weed and $150 in cash."

"OK," he said promptly as he pulled out a wad of cash and peeled me off $150. Then he gave me seven grams of weed in a sack. "All right, bro. I've got to get out of here. I'm meeting someone soon."

"OK. It was nice doing business with you," I said, pushing his car door open and getting out of the car. "Bye."

"Bye. Call me when you get more."

"Yep," I said.

As soon as I took one step, I could feel it. The world had changed. Everything was different. It felt good, though. I had forgotten all of my worries, fears, and memories. It seemed like everything was brighter. Mechanically, I walked to the car, opened the door, and jumped in. I took a second to think about what I was going to do next. I had plenty of time before I was going to meet up with Tammie. It was only 4:30 p.m., so I decided to go buy some clothes and take a shower. I went to Fred Meyer. Usually, I'd buy secondhand clothes, but not this time. I picked out some Levi's, a polo shirt, some boxers, some socks, and some tank tops. After buying them, I drove over to the Ballard

Public Pool. I was in the shower when I figured out my mistake. Damn. How could I have let Dave rip me off? I could answer this question with only one word: marijuana.

From then on, I made a point to never conduct business when I was stoned. How could I have been so stupid? He owed me $270 instead of $210. No wonder he was in such a hurry; he didn't want me to figure out his angle. He was infamous for being a shyster. I should have watched him more closely.

As soon as I got out of the shower and got dressed, I called him on the pay phone. No one answered, which seemed very convenient. I hated having to always be on my toes. I hated not being able to trust anyone. It was horrible. I remembered the trustworthy people my family used to go to church with. The characters I associated with now were all shady. They'd extort you in a minute and stab you in the back. It was a cold reality that I wasn't yet acclimated to. I had been too trusting.

After trying to call his number a few more times, I gave up. He wasn't going to answer. I called Tammie instead. I could trust her, right?

"Hello?" Tammie said.

"Hey, beautiful. It's me. I should be there in ten minutes."

"All right. I'll be outside."

"Cool. We're going to just walk around or something, right?"

"How come we can't roll around in your car?"

"I told you. It's not mine."

"What do you mean? You've got possession of it. Why can't we ride in it?"

"I'll explain when I see you."

"All right."

"I'll be there in a minute. Bye."

"Bye."

I was ashamed of the gradual escalation of my criminal activity. People accepted me still, but my work wasn't admirable or honorable. I wanted more for myself. I still do to this day.

As time went on, this hunger has never died. All of the past and future tragic events in my life couldn't stifle this desire, no matter how hard things got. I just didn't have the education or direction from positive role models to improve my situation, and this prevented me from achieving my dreams. I hope that these hindrances will be temporary.

I was not going to allow Tammie to ride in a stolen car with me. I would not be responsible for destroying her future with a criminal record. I wouldn't be able to live with myself if that happened. Hopping in the car, I started it up and pulled out of the parking lot. Driving was a new thrill. I loved it. Since I had learned to drive on my own, though, I was an incredibly unsafe driver. It didn't help that I was learning to drive in a stolen car. I drove recklessly, but I didn't know that at the time. I tended to drive really quickly and use the brakes too much. I did not pay attention to traffic on all sides of me. I got better as I got older, but it took a few accidents to get there. All of this could have been avoided if I had received adequate training.

I parked a block away from Tammie's apartment. There were not very many parking spaces in Fremont. This was probably due to the high number of apartment complexes in such a concentrated area.

When I was within twenty feet of her, I couldn't stop smiling. She was so beautiful. She was flawless. I still was amazed that she liked me. My insecurities always raised their ugly heads when I saw her.

"Baby, you look hot," I complimented her as I put my arms around her, hugged her, and gave her a long kiss.

"You look good too. I missed you," she pouted good-naturedly.

"What's been going on with you?"

"Not much, other than school, homework, school, and so on. It's the same stuff on different days."

"You need some excitement in your life," I said, pinching her butt.

"Oh!" she yelped, slapping my shoulder playfully. "Tell me, why can't we roll in your car?"

"It's not mine."

"I know that, but if you're borrowing a car, what's the difference if we go for a spin or not?"

"Do you want the truth or do you want the G-rated version?"

"The truth," she said.

"OK. It's not a borrowed car. It's stolen."

"What? Daniel! Now you're stealing cars?"

"Tammie, its December. I'd freeze to death if I didn't have shelter. Trust me, it's not something I'm proud of."

"Will you promise me something?"

"Yeah. What?"

"Will you please be careful?"

"Yes, I promise. With a hottie like you on my arm, why would I risk anything?" I said, pulling her into my arms and giving her a hug and a long kiss.

"I missed you too, babe. Even though I talk to you every day, I still miss you."

"I know. Me too."

"I want to buy you some dinner, but first let's get stoned."

"Sounds good."

"Do you have a bud pipe?"

"Yep. Here," she said, giving me her purple metal pipe.

"Awe. This is cute," I joked, pointing at the girlish color.

"Give it back! You can't be clowning on my pipe!" she said playfully.

"All right. I'm sorry."

"Fine. I accept your apology," she said, smiling.

"Here you go. Take a couple tokes and then pass it back," I said, handing her the bud-filled pipe.

"Thanks."

"It's my pleasure," I told her as we sought shelter in a covered bus stop. "Don't take too big of a toke. This is U-Dub bud."

"Oh. My favorite," she said as I blocked her so that no one saw her, and the wind did not affect her taking a toke. When she blew it out, she asked, "Where did you get it?" She asked too many questions, I thought.

"My friend Dave hooked me up."

"That's a lot of good weed. It must have cost you. How much did he charge you?"

"Um. It came out to about sixty bucks," I said, hoping she wouldn't continue interrogating me.

"Don't think I missed those new clothes either. Where did you get all that money? I want the truth!"

"Uh. Damn, Tammie! You ask too many questions."

"Yeah. Well, you don't have any parents looking out for you, so I guess I've got to. So tell me where you got it from."

"I don't want to tell you. I'm embarrassed."

"Come on. You can tell me anything."

"All right. I went car prowling," I said reluctantly.

"Car prowling? That's no worse than stealing cars. I don't like you doing any of it."

"I know. I'm just trying to survive. It's not easy, babe."

"I just hope you'll be safe. It's so dangerous. Do you know about all of the things that could go wrong? What happens if a cop tries to pull you over?"

"I'll try to get away."

"Exactly. That's what I'm talking about," she said with tears in her eyes. "I care about you, Daniel! I don't want to lose you."

"You're not going to lose me, babe," I said, grabbing her in a hug. It felt good to be wanted; I had missed that. I thought sadly about how I wished my parents felt this strongly about me. I didn't want to bring down our spirits, so I changed the subject. "You take a toke of bud and get all emotional," I said laughing.

"Whatever, Daniel. I just care."

"I know."

After eating some food, we spent the next couple of hours walking around, holding hands, and talking. I loved it. Being with her gave me a whirlwind of emotions. The time for her to go back home came quick. I hated that. Parting definitely brought me deep sorrow. I held her for what seemed like a minute, but was more like twenty minutes. Kissing her repeatedly, I finally peeled myself off of her. As we parted ways, we blew kisses and waved at each other. She took her key out and walked toward her building. I watched and made sure she got back into her apartment safely.

I never knew what would cause me to dwell on my past. Seeing her use a key did it that time. I remembered when I had a key to a home. David and I were both going to the Crown Hill Christian School, and we walked home on our own everyday. Our parents determined that we were old enough to have our own keys. They made it a big surprise ceremony. Both keys were attached to different key chains. David had a football keychain and I had a baseball keychain. We were both very happy. We felt like we were big kids, and we prized our keys. We acted like we had keys to our own house. Our parents seemed to be proud of us too. It was like they knew we were growing up quickly. It was like they felt like we were going to become lawyers or pilots someday. I felt sad to think about how much I had backslid since then. I hated myself. I felt like I must have done something to drive my parents to abandon me. Why else would they have abandoned me? I probably was the cause of their divorce too, I thought. I must have somehow been responsible for allowing that priest and John to abuse me. I found myself questioning everything. What am I really going to do? Am I going to be homeless for the rest of my life? I didn't know. I was confused. I didn't have anyone to turn to. Nobody truly cared about me. Sure, Tammie was there, but I would never unload all of my hopelessness onto her. That would be unfair. I didn't know how she would respond. I couldn't do that. I only wanted my parents to be there for me, to talk to me, to hold me, to let me cry on their shoulders, and to provide for me. I would have done anything for that.

I couldn't stand being alone, so I called Jerry's house and inquired about what they were up to. I needed some company. I was feeling too lonely, sad, and hopeless.

"Hello," somebody answered.

"Hey, what's up? This is Daniel. Who's this?"

"What's up, Daniel. It's Ton."

"Hi. What are you guys doing?"

"We're just about to go to Gasworks Park."

"What? I'm in Fremont right now. I just left Tammies's."

"Tammie? Do you mean my sister's friend?"

"Yep."

"I heard you were messing with her. She's got big tits. I'd like to kiss on them."

"Hey! Don't be talking about my woman like that!"

"What are you going to do?"

"Just respect my woman. She isn't a tramp."

"All I'm saying is I'd like to hump her."

"Screw you, Ton!"

"I'd like to screw Tammie."

"Forget you. I'm hanging up," I said angrily.

"Hold up. I need your help."

"For what?"

"Just meet me at Gasworks."

"Fine," I said. "But promise me you won't keep talking about my woman like that."

"I promise. For the record, all women are tramps."

"No they're not! There are faithful women and there are promiscuous women."

"Whatever. You're just whipped."

"How long will it take for you to get to Gasworks?"

"We're leaving right now. We'll probably be there in fifteen minutes."

"All right. I'll be by the bathrooms."

"Cool. Later."

"Bye."

I was disgusted by the way he talked about women. He always talked like that. I think he felt insecure about his own inadequacies. He knew he could get a rise out of me by talking that way about Tammie. I found myself deeply wishing I had true friends who would never want to hustle you, harass you, rob you, or take advantage of you.

I left the car where it was, walked down to the 7-Eleven convenience store, and bought a warm cup of coffee. I put all of the fixings in my coffee: Irish cream, sugar, and milk. It was perfect. It gave me the caffeine that I needed, and it kept my hands and my insides warm.

When I walked down to Gasworks Park, I chose to take the long route. I had time to waste. I ended up passing the Red Hook Brewery, which had kegs of beer just sitting out in the open. I thought about how I could easily grab a couple pony kegs or a horse keg. I filed this information away in my memory banks. I might need to grab a keg someday.

By the time I got to Gasworks it was 9:30 p.m. nobody was there yet, so I decided to walk around the pipes. I could still see the bathrooms, so I wouldn't miss them. Maybe it was as a sign of my bad luck, but a big pile of white bird poop dropped on me from above. I cursed aloud.

"Great," I thought. "What's next?"

Hurriedly, I ran out of the covered area. I didn't want to get pooped on again. In the bathroom, I cleaned the poop off. As I was doing this, Ton came in with Ike and a couple guys I didn't know.

"What's up, Daniel? What happened to your coat?" Ton asked.

"A bird pooped on it!"

"That's probably what they thought of you," said Ton laughing.

"Yeah. I'm sure they think a lot more than you do," I said laughing back.

"Screw you," he said defensively.

"Oh, you can dish it but can't take it?"

"All right. Let's quit clowning. It's time to be serious," Ton said, looking at a guy with long hair, goatee and a Metallica t-shirt who was walking toward us. He had to be six or seven years older than me. "Hey buddy!"

"Hello. Where do you want to do this?" the newcomer said.

"In the bathroom. Come on." Ton said, pointing for us to stand in front of the bathroom door.

"I hope this is good acid."

Acid? I had never done acid and I didn't want to do it. I could barely see between Ike and the other two guys. It looked like they were blocking the doorway to prevent someone from getting out.

"No," I thought. "I must be tripping. This is just a drug deal, but why would he need my help if that were the case?" Then I got my answer.

"This is a jack move," Ton said as he punched the newcomer with all that he had.

"Help! Help!" The newcomer screamed, frantically trying to wrestle and scramble out of the bathroom. His screaming must have paralyzed Ton, Ike, and the other two guys. Unintentionally, they allowed him to slip through. He screamed as if he were dying. He struggled relentlessly through their clutch. At one point, he was within inches of me. I could have easily grabbed him, but I didn't. Forget that. I didn't want any part in this. Once the guy started gaining some distance from his robbers, he quit screaming. His screaming continued in my head, though. I was bothered by it. I could not bear it. I was going to run to the stolen car.

Ton yelled, "Come on! We've got to get out of here!"

He was right. My stolen car was parked blocks away. By the time I would have gotten there, the cops would have been swarming the area, so I followed Ton and the other guys and jumped in their car. When we were entrenched in the suburban maze of side streets, I asked what had happened.

"Why did you do that?" I asked loudly.

"We wanted his acid! Why else?" Ton responded arrogantly.

"You should have told me beforehand! I wouldn't have wanted anything to do with it and you know that!"

"I needed one more body to block him from getting out."

"That's crap and you know it," I said.

The reality of the matter was that I detested violent crime. Throughout my years on the streets, I avoided that type of activity. When it involves self-defense I think that violence is acceptable, but in general I would much rather be stealing. Many people think that there is no distinction between violence and self-defense, but to me there is a big difference. As I said before, my victims were corporations. They were abstract and I did not face them. This contributed greatly to my mental state. My mentality was obviously wrong, but my needs made me overcome all abstract constructions. All I knew were my tangible needs: hunger, shelter, comfort, etc. These needs were what propelled me to act lawlessly.

With the robbery foiled, Ton wanted to go car prowling. I had reservations about this, but nevertheless I decided to join him. I didn't have many other options. It was late at night. We had ended up at Jerry's place. My stolen car was still parked in Fremont, which was a few miles away.

"All right. I'll go car prowling with you, but we'll share everything fifty-fifty, right?"

"Yeah."

"OK."

After wasting a couple of hours, we headed out on foot. We pillaged the apartments between 105th and 85th off of Greenwood Avenue. Ton preferred underground garages. They housed many cars and they were effectively noise proof, so it wasn't a problem to make a racket pulling a stereo. Moreover, apartment buildings housed younger tenants, who were more likely to have nice stereo systems. My ability to car prowl was amateurish. Ton was an expert. So, I was designated the point man. Like I had done with Nathan, I would watch out for him and make sure that no one caught him in the act. This was fine with me. It gave me the opportunity to learn more about car prowling. This was shameful but true.

Perhaps in some cosmic gesture of karma, an unknown car owner set Ton up. It happened while he was in a Honda Accord. He had just taken the radio player out. Afterward, he popped open the trunk. There was no stereo equipment, but there was a nice big jug of Welch's grape juice. Exhausted from the tireless efforts, he readily twisted the top to take a nice long gulp.

"Ah!" He spat, spewing dark liquid out of his blackened mouth.

"What's wrong?" I asked apprehensively.

"It's oil!" he cried. Someone had put used oil in the bottle.

I couldn't help myself. I busted up laughing. The look on his face was priceless. He must have taken a couple of swigs of it. The oil spilled down his chin thickly. It was hilarious. In my book, he deserved it. Maybe I deserved bad things to happen to me too. I constantly questioned myself. I wondered if bad things had happened to me because I had deserved them. Why else would they have happened? Who could I blame except for myself?

By the end of the night, we had accumulated a trove of stereo equipment. We brought it all back to Jerry's place. From there, we called Dave. He came over and cashed us out. I was able to recover the rest of what he owed me. Altogether, I walked away with a little over two hundred dollars. With the pot split between us, what Dave owed me, resulted in me walking away with a cool three hundred dollars. It was not bad for a night's work.

I left Jerry's house and took the bus back to Fremont, where I grabbed the car that I had stolen. My fatigued body was protesting. It did not want to continue. It was too tired. My eyelids exhibited this feeling of exhaustion. They drooped heavily, and it was hard to keep them up. Every time the bus stopped, I had to open my eyes so that I would not tilt forward haphazardly. It was a struggle that I ultimately succumbed to.

By the time the bus reached Fremont, I had passed out. I missed my exit. The bus was downtown before I realized it. Quickly, I pulled the buzzer and hopped out at the next stop. It took thirty minutes for me to catch another bus going back the other way. "Just my luck," I thought. Shivering in the cold, I thankfully managed to stay awake.

I didn't want to miss my exit again, so I forced myself to stay awake on the bus. I made it back to the car successfully. Before getting into the car, I scoped the area out. I didn't want to jump into a car that was being staked out. Luckily, it wasn't. I got in quickly and started it up. Pulling out was difficult. I was boxed in. Parking in Fremont was such a headache. Inch by incremental inch, I finally managed to maneuver out of the parking spot.

Since it was December, I would get cold sleeping in the car. Driving to a thrift store, I picked up a warm sleeping bag to use whenever I slept in the car. It was only ten dollars, so it was worth it. After going to the thrift store, I parked in an isolated location and promptly passed out.

I spent the next couple of weeks living off of the money that I had already generated. Whenever it was possible, I stretched every dollar. I did not like committing crimes. I struggled greatly with it, so I tried to be as frugal as possible. Obviously, I had to spend money on basic necessities: food, hygiene products, showers, etc. For the most part, though, I remained extremely conservative with my funds. With Tammie, I put up a facade of robust financial strength. I'd pick flowers for her, wrap them in nice paper, and present them in glamorous fashion. Who knows if she noticed that they were store-bought or not. I had to be aware of my resources, but I also wanted to have nice things. Moreover, I got pleasure out of giving nice things to people, so it was a constant battle. I found myself falling into the practice of trying to buy friends. I did it routinely throughout my childhood and into adulthood, so it was a trait that I was well aware of. I would always share my last dollar. Some people took advantage of this. I couldn't help it, though. I thought that that was what friends did. At my core, I am big-hearted. The problem, however, was that I shared my generosity with people who did not appreciate me, care for me, or otherwise remember my kindness. Instead, they would forget my generosity immediately. My generosity was wasted on people who would prey on me like I was any other victim. If the need were to arise, they would not hesitate to take advantage of me. I know this now, but at the time I thought that that was what friends did.

Today, I remain relatively pragmatic about my characteristics. I can dissect them rather effectively. On a clinical level, it is clear that I have suffered irreversible mental health problems. I know this from psychologist reports and from my own conclusions. Remarkably and thankfully, I do not have any sexual deviances. However, since I was subjected to abandonment, sexual abuse, homelessness, criminality, and violence during my formative years, I was practically guaranteed to have some mental health problems. I know that now. This understanding has caused me to endeavor to address these issues. Instead of using medication, I try to cognitively isolate my mental distortions and actively work at changing them. Once I've determined the distortion, I attempt to change it by a few different methods. For example, when I think negative thoughts, I separate them. I write them down and spend time disproving them. I also find other ways to remedy these negative thoughts. I arrived at this strategy for cognitive metamorphosis after many years of having illogical and nonsensical misconceptions, misjudgments, blunders, and errors. Regrettably, I arrived at this transformative strategy too late to avoid my encounters with the law. This has been my journey through life. I am sharing it with you in good faith and with clean hands. My goal is to delineate the tragic events that shaped me, fueled my disintegration, and prevented me from being the person I wanted to be and still want to become. I want to become a productive member of society, but I have a long way to go. I hope that these books will help me move forward with my recovery and my redemption. I think that they will. It is highly therapeutic for me to share my deepest thoughts, emotions, actions, and secrets. It gives me consolation to know that I am no longer the sole confidant. It helps to know that I have unloaded my burden to an extent. I am entrusting it to you, so please respect it, share it, and use it to help others. I am only one person, and I need you. Together, we can spread the message about how traumatic events can destroy a child's future.

This book takes place when I was fourteen years old, but now I am much older. I can state with genuine candor that life has been very hard for me. I hope that I can articulate the anguish that I have gone through. You have yet to read about all of the disasters that I went through, but I hope that you will join me on this monumental undertaking. To me, this book is more than a labor of love or a cleansing of my soul. I represent all victims of abandonment, sexual abuse, and violence, and I trust that my story is universal.

I would be doing everyone a disservice if I did not discuss mental health, crime, and the criminal justice system. I am an authority on the topic because of my experience on the receiving end of these issues. People with severe mental health problems can escape psychological examinations and treatment even after they have been imprisoned numerous times. Unless you are smearing feces on the wall, talking to yourself, or mutilating yourself, you will not get adequate care. This fact scares me and it should scare you too. Some of the most demented souls are released from prisons all across the country daily. These individuals have warped thought processes that can be cured and changed. They need help, however, to change this, but they aren't getting it. Instead, the legal system releases them untreated. This sets them up for the kind of failure that I experienced. These people assuredly gravitate toward crime, violence, ill-defined causes, extremist views, and radicalization of some sort. In this era of unlimited information, it is easy for these individuals to find materials that support their extremist views. They can surround themselves with this material and not learn about opposing views. They entrench themselves. No one will be able to dissuade them from their causes. These causes often include a variety of agendas. They focus on patriotic, environmental, and religious issues. The list is endless. Left untreated, these agendas can transform people into extremists, radicals, and terrorists. We should not allow this to happen. America is familiar with preventative care. We already have preventative medical and dental care; we should also have preventative care for mental health. This is especially true for foster kids. During the 2012 Do Something Awards on VH1, I learned that 80 percent of foster kids end up in the judicial system. This is unacceptable. We can do something about this if we recognize the problem and then work to solve it. We are allowing good children to fall into this default setting. By default, they are repeatedly incarcerated. This is a tragedy, but can it be solved? I don't know. It will take brighter minds than mine to address this issue, but the first step needs to be taken. Who will take this step? I don't know. It could be you. Anybody can dedicate his or her life to the foster kids of today. That's where it starts. I sincerely hope that my disclosures will in some small way stoke a wildfire of change. It can happen. It is not an impossible feat. It will take time, energy, resources, compassion, and forgiveness, but it can be done.

Forgiveness is significant for me. I have had to own up to the crimes that I committed. I have allowed my sense of pain and hopelessness to manifest itself in so many different ways. As

I further describe the events of my life, you will witness these manifestations. I truly wish that I could detail every crime and victim. I would love to find closure by having my victims forgive me, but that would not be fair to them, since they need their privacy. In each book, I freely offer an open-ended, unconditional apology from my heart. I hope that my victims will accept my apology.

As Christmas approached, I did everything I could to not think about it. I would act like I was indifferent to it. I looked like Scrooge, and I didn't want others to know that I was heartbroken. I think that I hid it pretty well. If anyone had noticed how bad I felt, I doubt they would have cared. Why should they? I was nobody. Christmas Eve was very hard for me. All of my acquaintances were busy with their families, and nobody had invited me anywhere. This wasn't a surprise. I cuddled up in the stolen car with magazines and a book. I had also bought groceries to eat throughout the holidays. I did not want to risk not being able to find a store open at Christmas, so I shopped ahead of time.

I lay in the warm sleeping bag in the back seat and strained desperately to not let my thoughts run wild. It was pointless. My thoughts strayed. I saw Christmas lights and this made me think about my family's Christmas rituals. Every year, we would decorate the house, put up Christmas lights, and make gingerbread cookies. With a needle, some thread, and some popcorn, we made streamers for the Christmas tree. We did all of this as a family. I missed this so much. On Christmas night, we would put a plate that was full of cookies and a cup of milk out for Santa Claus. One year, David had the responsibility of making the cookies. He directed me and our other younger siblings to do different tasks, such as stirring, breaking the eggs, pouring the batter, and keeping time. Once we put the cookies in to bake, we all used our fingers to lick the delightful batter. When we were done, David was furious with me. I had stolen a cookie from his Santa

Claus plates. I didn't think that he had been paying attention, but he had been. He stormed at me and slapped the cookie out of my hand. I was shocked by his outburst. All I could do was turn around and run away. I remembered this fondly. That's what family did; we bickered but we loved each other. I missed the good times and the bad times equally. Both of these extremes represented family life. I would have done anything to get that back, but it was gone forever. That hurt me so much.

"Why did this happen to our family?" I screamed aloud, throwing the magazine violently. "I hate my life!" I yelled as a tear dropped down my cheek. "I can't take this!" I sobbed.

I needed some cold air to jar me from my melancholy. Opening the car door and sniffing the air, I decided to walk for a while. No one was out on the streets. I was alone and this was a good thing. I didn't want anyone to see me like this. Walking seemed to keep my troubled mind occupied. Then I treaded past a big house near Sandel Park. The house had a large bay window. Christmas lights surrounded the window and the house. Inside the house, I saw a big, brightly lit Christmas tree. I could see a grand table in the dining room that was filled with food. There was a turkey. I also saw ham, yams, mashed potatoes, and cranberry sauce. I loved cranberry sauce. This family of four was sitting expansively at the table. They looked so happy and cheerful. I spent ten minutes on that sidewalk as the snow fell heavily on me. I didn't care, though. This family enthralled me. I would have done anything to have a family like that again. They looked so peaceful and so serene. More than anything in the world, I wanted to live like them. Heartbreakingly, I gazed at them like a kid looking at a puppy through a window. They were oblivious to my presence. They were too caught up in their own bliss. I could not stop crying tears of longing, desire, and yearning. I craved this kind of family life and love. It meant so much more to me now. "Why, Lord Jesus? Why?" I lamented loudly. "Please give me back my family, Lord." Exasperated, I kicked a tree and some piles of snow tempestuously. Depleted and despondent, I collapsed onto the ground.

CHAPTER 9

I agonized over my desolation. I knew then that I needed to fortify myself. I had to adapt to my new reality. It wasn't going to be simple, painless, or easy, but I had to adjust. I could not break down on every holiday. That would not do me any good. It would just depress me. I promised myself that I would not do this anymore.

On Christmas Day, I called Tammie to wish her a merry Christmas. I didn't have anyone else to call.

"Hello," Tammie answered cheerfully.

"Merry Christmas, beautiful!"

"Hey! Merry Christmas to you too, baby."

"What are you up to?"

"Not much. I'm just doing the family thing."

"Oh. Did you get anything cool?" I asked.

"Yeah. I got a nice coat, some shoes, and a purse. I needed a purse, so it came at a good time. Anyway, what's up with you? Are you OK?"

"Yeah. I'm OK."

"Daniel, I know it's got to be hard for you."

"It isn't a big deal," I said.

"Sure. You know I'm here for you, right?"

"Yeah. I know that."

I did know this, but it was hard for me to let anyone in, especially Tammie. I was more preoccupied with impressing her. I couldn't unload my baggage. Forget that. I spent the rest of the night listening to the radio and smoking marijuana. I indulged excessively. It was the only thing I could do to keep my troubled mind from wandering off. No matter how hard I tried, I could not take my mind off of my family. Where were my siblings? How were they? I had not seen them in months. I hoped that they were OK. I was sure that they were taken care of, but I still wanted to ease my mind by talking to them.

It hurt me deeply that I couldn't even call them, see them, or write to them. I missed them terribly. I wondered if they missed me. I am positive that my rapid transition into using marijuana was due to the powerful emotions that were coursing through me. I dwelled on countless emotions. I only found solace, comfort, and relief in numbing my emotions and blunting their potency. Maybe this was wrong, but I did not know how else to dull their impact on my mind and on my life.

CHAPTER 10

A few days after Christmas, I ran into Ton at Jerry's again. As always, he was being obnoxious. He seemed to always find something to tease me about. I was always the butt of his wisecracks. I was an easy target. It was hard to barb him back because he would just get defensive and use his size against me. I hated that. I wished I were his size. This would have at least given me a fighting chance. He was criticizing me over the way I pronounced my alias. Apparently, I said it without being commanding. He railed on me about it, mocking me terribly.

"Since you've got a warrant out for your arrest, what alias will you use if the cops ask what your name is?"

"I'll say I'm Danny Mulloy!"

"I'll say I'm Danny Mulloy," he jeered.

"What's so funny about that?"

"Danny Mulloy," he mocked me in a girlish voice.

"Whatever," I said as I walked away.

"Danny Mulloy," he sneered, following me.

Their ridicule went on for an extended amount of time. He

found it amusing. It gave him something to heckle me about. It was hard to not take his bait. If I had argued any further with him, he would have just escalated his taunting. He always disguised his put-downs as friendly ribbing. Back then I just chalked it up as him being jovial, but I can now see through that. Later that evening, he disclosed his intentions for the night. He wanted to go car prowling, and he needed me to watch his back.

"Come on, Daniel!"

"I don't know, Ton. I'm not feeling up to it."

"I need you."

"You can go by yourself. I've done it by myself before."

"I know but I also want a car."

"You're going to steal a car?"

"Yep."

"What kind?"

"I don't know but will you come? I hate doing it blind."

"Uh. All right but I've got reservations."

"Reservations?"

"Yeah. I've got a weird feeling."

"Well, get over it."

"OK. I'll try."

We set off for the Ballard area. Once we got there, we hit a number of cars. Two of the cars had full-blown stereo systems with nice pullouts, amplifiers, and speaker boxes. We hid the stereo system in the bushes, planning to come back for it later. This was a common practice that alleviated the burden of lugging it all around.

Trudging down the dark streets, we searched earnestly for a car to swipe. The cars with the most potential were always hard to get. They would have car alarms. They would be parked on a busy street or close to the owner's house. It seemed like we might not be able to acquire one.

By dawn, the prospect of getting a car was looking bleak. Feeling forlorn, we stalked around voraciously. Bent on procuring a car at all costs, our cautiousness diminished significantly. Soon, people would be walking around. We had to locate one. Turning a corner, we both noticed a car at the same time. It was a Chevy Blazer in a covered parking spot. The carport was below an apartment. The bedroom window was directly above the Blazer. This alarmed me. It was risky to be so close to the car owner's bedroom. One loud noise could rouse the owner. This put us in a precarious position. Nevertheless, we were determined to get it. Furtively, we walked over to the car. It was locked. Ton quickly produced the flathead screwdriver and began digging the lock out. Within a minute, he was in the car. Hastily, he began the process of starting the car.

The crunching, cracking, and snapping noises that Ton was making made me tense, but I had to overcome my uneasiness. I couldn't allow my anxieties to interfere with my task of being the lookout. If left unchecked, my uneasiness could easily hamper my abilities. I couldn't let this happen. I tuned all of my senses to the surrounding area. I did not detect anything of concern. Ton extended his finger and gave me the universal sign to come to him. He needed help breaking the lock on the steering wheel. We jointly twisted it back and forth until it moved unencumbered. Ton then started the car and we pulled out of the carport. What I saw next frightened me. A man hastily parted the bedroom curtains and looked down at us. He was clearly distraught. Ton thought that this was funny, and he waved to him. "What a jerk," I thought. He didn't need to do that, but that was the type of cretin that Ton was. He was a real goon. No doubt, the guy would be calling the police. We could not stay in this car.

"We have to ditch this car," I said frantically.

"No we don't. We need to get our loot first."

"Ton. The cops are going to be swarming the area really soon."

"So what. Let's get the goods. We'll be all right." He really believed this. I wanted to believe it too. We loaded the goods hurriedly into the car. Then we stealthily drove through the back streets and alleys until we were far from the apartment. As if the distance would extinguish the possibility of a cop recognizing the car, Ton lowered his vigilance. What a fool. He was a regular imbecile. Instead of continuing to drive along the back roads, we drifted to the busy thoroughfare of Greenwood Avenue. With the music blaring, Ton bobbed his head along with the tune. He must have been relishing his sage elusiveness. He was visibly happy. I turned the music down.

"Where are you going?" I asked.

"I'm going to call Dave and sell this stereo equipment."

"Cool. What store are you going to?"

"I'm going to the convenience store on 145th and Greenwood."

"I don't like being on this busy street."

"We're good. The cops aren't looking for us in this neighborhood."

"Yeah, but we are still in Seattle."

"Quit being negative."

"All I'm saying is that we should still be on our toes."

He pulled up next to a pay phone in the convenience store parking lot. As we were walking to the store, Ton got behind me and kicked my foot, causing me to fall. He laughed.

"Watch where you're going, stupid," he scoffed.

"Why'd you do that?" I asked indignantly, picking myself up and brushing off.

"You're a jerk, you know that!"

"Yeah. So what? You're not going to do nothing about it," he said, smirking cruelly.

While I was growing up, my so-called friends mistreated me. This happened a lot on the streets for a variety of reasons. For one, I craved acceptance. My self-esteem was so low that I took whatever these so-called friends dished out. If a stranger had inflicted this type of judgment on me, I wouldn't have accepted it. These so-called friends gave me just the right amount of camaraderie, acceptance, commiseration, and tutelage on moneymaking enterprises. When I look back to those days when my friends treated me poorly, I feel nauseous. I can't believe I took their abuse. In some ways, I liken it to being hazed. I was the community punching bag. If it had been limited to the mistreatment I've described so far, it wouldn't have been such a big deal. It would have just been a part of growing up. But things got much worse. Notably, I had escaped the abuse at the group home only to place myself in a different type of danger and abuse. I had become involved in homelessness, criminality, violence, and malnourishment, but I wasn't too worried. I was stuck in the present moment. I only worried about what I had to do to find food and places to sleep.

This was a grave mistake, and I'm still paying for it to this day. Regrettably, I have struggled to escape the repercussion of my formative years. While my criminal record has definitely hobbled me, those years also tarnished the way I view things and interact with people. To this day, I have immense self-esteem problems that are hard to overcome. Unless I'm comfortable and familiar with someone, it is difficult for me to look him or her in the eyes and not stutter. I get too nervous. I recognize it for what it is now. I am self-conscious, insecure, and distrustful. These attributes have all played a part in my development.

After calling Dave and buying some snacks, we went back to the car. Then we pulled back out onto Greenwood Avenue. It was typically a busy thoroughfare, but at the moment there was little traffic. It was very early. Although the sun was coming up, the street was still not fully active yet. Ton was still bobbing his head to the loud music when I saw the predator. My worse fear was coming true. It was a Seattle police officer. As soon as I saw him, my stomach churned and did somersaults. Ton was still bobbing his fat head ignorantly. I swiftly turned the radio down, and Ton finally noticed the cop.

"Crap!" he gasped.

"Just be cool," I told him, watching the cop. "Damn. He's turning around! What are we going to do?"

"I need you to do me a big favor, Daniel."

"What?" I demanded as the cop turned his lights and sirens on.

"There's no reason we both should go down for this. You've got a warrant out for your arrest anyway, and you're a juvenile. You'll only get a slap on your wrist. Will you say that you stole the car and let me drive it?" He implored feverishly.

"What? I don't know, Ton." I demurred.

"Come on. Please. If I get arrested, I'll go to the adult jail." He pleaded as he was pulled over.

"How come you're not at least trying to elude him?" I queried.

"This car doesn't have guts," he replied. It looked more like Ton himself didn't have any guts.

"All right, man. I'll take the rap," I agreed idiotically. My callow and loyal nature had gotten the better of me.

"Driver, put your hands out the window. Nice and slow," said the officer over the bullhorn. Ton readily complied. He looked like a doe in the headlights. "OK. Driver, slowly use one hand to open the door. Then come out with your hands up and lie on the ground." Ton eagerly complied. The cop repeated this procedure with me. As soon as we were both on the ground, the officers jumped on us, roughly planting their knees into our backs. When the cop was cuffing me, I looked around pensively and sadly.

I was going back to juvie, though I did not know how long I would be there for. What I did know, however, was that I'd be gone for at least a few months. This gave me the blues. I gazed at the trees, the cars, the houses, and the birds as if I wouldn't see them again. I wouldn't see them again until I had completed my sentence.

Most kids in my shoes wouldn't even have spent a week in juvie. They would have gotten probation. I, on the other hand, would spend months in there. I had no one to call and no one to claim me. If I had, I wouldn't have been in that stolen car to begin with. This was a typical catch-22. The kids who needed the most help, guidance, and aid were the ones who were locked up for the longest amount of time and treated the worst. It felt like kids in two-parent homes were more important and forgivable than me. I hated that.

The cop jerked me to my feet. He grunted, pushed me toward his cruiser, opened the door to the back seat, and catapulted me into the car. I landed swiftly on the hard plastic. I could almost hear the cop musing to himself, "You're nothing but a punk kid, a good-for-nothing troublemaker, and a rebel."

I don't blame him. He didn't know anything about me, my story, or my plight. All he knew about was my criminal act, and that was enough for him. He didn't want to know any more than my vital statistics, my date of birth, my name, and my address. After some cursory questions, I lied and said that I had stolen the car. I said that Ton hadn't known that I had stolen in. The cop ate it all up. He was more than happy to place the blame on me without asking any further questions.

That is very funny to me now. He didn't even question the obvious. It was clear that the older adult had pressured me into confessing. "Good police work, guy," I thought. The officer drove me to the North Precinct. The one-story building was fortified with thick glass. The locked doors required someone to buzz you in, and there were holding cells and cubicles for investigators. The building was within blocks of the Northgate Mall.

The Northgate Mall, I recalled nostalgically, was the closest one to my childhood home. Dennis and I would ride our bikes there, trekking laboriously up and down the hills, talking jocularly, and playfully discussing this or that. I had been so careless and innocent then. I had been oblivious to the rough reality of life and the brewing events that would haunt the rest of my life. This one particular time, we saved up money so that we could see a movie at the theater. It was called *The Last Action Hero*, and it starred Arnold Schwarzenegger. The plot is still vivid in my mind. Arnold Schwarzenegger was my hero, but things have changed considerably since then.

CHAPTER 11

The authority figures transported me to the King County Juvenile Detention Center in a fortified mini-van. They handcuffed me and three other individuals. They then shackled us and herded us into this paddy wagon. There were two windows in the back that were about the size of my hand. They were fogged over. The stench of puke permeated the holding pen. It was disgusting.

Ironically, I had never been sent to detention when I was in school, yet I was entering this juvenile facility for the third time. It was a big leap. I had always been a good student. I never gave my teachers any problems. Most of them couldn't pick me up in a line-up if their lives depended on it. I was so quiet, attentive, and unassuming that I easily coasted through their classes without much notice.

If any teachers or past acquaintances noticed anything special about me, it would be my smile. I had a brilliant smile. I used to smile at everyone. Smiling came easy. I was so happy-go-lucky. To this day, I occasionally flash that smile. I'm not in a very cheery

A picture of Daniel (in his mom's arms), his parents Robert & Karen., and his brother David. From top left is Robert and Karen, Daniel, David, Kristine, Dennis, and Doug. This was the family's last picture together.

This is Daniel's childhood home. The years have changed it very little. Even the basketball hoop his father made is still attached to the carport.

This would be the last school photo Daniel ever took. He was in the sixth grade.

This is the fosterhome Daniel was dropped off at. Which
at the time belonged to Mike & Jill.

The entrance to Sandel Park.

There was a wood bench that jutted out from this building and that is where Daniel spent his first night homeless. At Sandel Park.

The kiddie pool at Sandel Park.

Here is an imposing view of the Auburn House Group
Home.

Here is a long view of the Auburn House Group Home.

environment these days, so this doesn't happen very often.

As you'll discover in this trilogy, I haven't been happy for a long time. It has been quite the odyssey. Calamities and catastrophic misfortunes have scarred me immensely. I felt wretched as I entered the juvenile detention facility again. It seemed like a gray cloud of gloom was engulfing my world. The familiar surroundings did not blunt my dismal feelings. Although I had been there three times, none of the staff members knew me, and I did not know any of the kids. The facility itself had not changed very much. It was the same drab establishment that it had been before. The only noticeable difference involved the programming. They had implemented a meritocracy. They would only promote the kids who stayed on their best behavior, followed all of the rules, and did their assigned chores. There were four levels. All of the kids automatically started at level two. Level one was the lowest rung. They reserved it for kids who had been demoted because they had misbehaved, gotten in a fight, or destroyed something. Unless they were let out for school, meals, or showers, kids in the lowest rung were confined to their cells. Kids in level two got to spend more time outside of their cells. They got to go outside to the yard or to the gym. Kids at each level were able to buy set amounts of stuff from the commissary. However, they did not allow kids to spend their own money. We each received a set stipend. The amount that each kid received varied depending on his or her level. Level one got $2.50. Level two got five dollars. Level three got ten dollars. Level four got fifteen dollars. Because of this system, kids strived earnestly to be promoted to the next level.

That was the only way for us to get candy. I do not know who came up with the stipend policy, but it definitely made a difference for kids who had no outside aid. When I had been here before, it had been hard to watch the kids with outside support getting big sacks of commissary items. I lacked the funds to buy even a bar of soap. They would supply indigent kids with these small bars of soap like they had at hotels. They were terrible. They smelled like chemicals and dried your skin out. They caused me to break out. Even worse, they only provided three bars of soap per week. The soap never lasted that long. By the middle of the week the soap was gone. I would have to reuse discarded slivers of soap. It was degrading and humiliating. I usually made a deal with a kid who had money. I would trade my food for a bar of Irish Spring soap. I remember that Irish Spring soap smelled so refreshing. It was amazing. Because of my destitution, I appreciated the most basic things. Among other things, I appreciated being clean and eating candy. These things meant so much more to me at that point than they ever had before. I willingly starved myself to get a bar of that precious Irish Spring soap. It was pathetic. I was so used to going without food, though, so it wasn't a big deal. This, at least, was what I told myself.

Kids who were at level two and above were allowed to go to church services on Sunday nights. Even kids who weren't Christians wanted to go. Beyond getting to leave their pods, they'd get to see the girls. This was huge for teenage boys; it was like going to a school dance.

Regrettably, I don't know what school dances feel like, so I'm only speculating. I would sometimes imagine myself taking a beautiful girl to a dance. I especially dreamed of prom. I heard all of these tales about it. I envisioned it being like a fairy tale. I would have done anything to experience it, but that wasn't in my cards. I do, however, wonder if I would have been a wallflower. Maybe I would have been the outgoing popular kid who smoothly sidled up to his homecoming queen. Maybe I would have been the mischievous kid who spikes the punch bowl. It is impossible to know.

Kids who were at level three got to spend more time outside of their cells at night. They got to stay out until 9 p.m. Kids who were at level two had to come in at 8 p.m. The fourth level was the premium level. It was the top of the line. In addition to going to the commissary and spending time outside of their cells, these kids got to go to the pod where the girls stayed. It was cool. They were allowed to play card games with them, such as Monopoly and Sorry. I highly doubt that the boys or the girls were thinking about games. I heard some interesting stories about how they would sneak a kiss or a touch.

I never made it to level four. It seemed like something was always stopping me. I was always fighting or getting into trouble. It took ninety days for a kid to make it to level four. My longest stay in the juvie was three and a half months, which was 105 days.

I was held in juvenile detention for seventy days on this trip. After this stay, I went to the juvenile institution. There was no reason for me to prolong my stay. The majority of the kids did just that, but they had family and friends who would come to visit them. I didn't have this luxury. I used to daydream about my mom and dad coming to visit me. I would have run into their arms and screamed. In sign language, I would have begged for forgiveness. I would have apologized profusely and asked for one more chance. I would have repented for anything that they wanted me to repent for, regardless of whether or not I had done anything. This would never happen, though. I was sadly on my own. My situation with Tammie drove this point home. As soon as I was settled into juvie, I wrote to her daily. After two weeks, I still had not heard from her. This worried me. Why wouldn't she write to me? There must be something wrong. I did not have anyone to call who could help me find out what had happened. This was hard. My young heart pined for her. She did not write to me, and I did not know why. Maybe she was too busy. Maybe she had moved. Maybe she had not received my letters for some reason. I couldn't stop thinking about it. I knew that she knew that I was incarcerated. Ton would have told his sister, Maria, and she would have told Tammie. While I was incarcerated, there was no way for me to know why she had stopped contacting me. I would have to wait, even though it was extremely difficult. To distract myself, I created a routine that I could follow mindlessly. This gave me solace and comfort. It soothed my wandering mind. I plotted every hour of every day from the moment I woke up. I planned when I would eat breakfast, lunch, and dinner. I planned my schedule for working out. I designed rigorous drills so that I would grow fatigued. It worked. I would do all of the standard exercises: push-ups, pull-ups, dips, and sit-ups. For cardio, I would play basketball. I topped all of this off with burpees, bear crawls, and sprints. A kid who lived a couple of cells down from me introduced me to these exhaustive drills. His name was Dustin. He and I clicked immediately. We were the only two white kids in the pod, but that wasn't the only reason we got along. He was three years older than me, but he didn't act like this bothered him. I liked that. The topics of our conversations varied. He was in for multiple burglaries. His parents came to visit him regularly. I wondered why he had committed these burglaries in the first place.

"Hey, Dustin," I gasped after our workout. We were sitting up against the wall, sweating and breathing hard.

"Yeah," he panted.

"Why do you rob houses? I'm curious. You've got two parents who love you and shelter you. Why risk that and come here?" I asked.

"Well, I did my first burglary on a whim. I had just turned sixteen. My parents couldn't afford to buy me a car, and I wanted one badly. My family isn't exactly dirt poor, but we do struggle. My dad is the only one who works. He does construction. He stretches his paycheck to provide for me and my other three siblings. I didn't even have the nerve to ask for a car."

"So, you did burglaries to buy a car?"

"At first, yeah."

"Did you ever get a car?"

"Yep. I got a drop-top Mustang convertible," he said boastfully.

"Wow! How long did it take for you to buy it?"

"One week."

"One week? It must have cost you thousands."

"It cost me $8, 999," he said.

"Dang. After you bought it, why didn't you stop doing burglaries?"

"The money was too good. I was able to buy whatever I wanted and go anywhere."

"Didn't your parents wonder how you had bought the car?"

"Yeah, but I told them I was selling weed."

"Your parents accepted that?"

"Yep. I've been smoking weed since I was fourteen."

"That's crazy. Is this your first time here?"

"Nope. I was here a couple months ago. My parents came to the court hearings, and the court let my parents take me."

"That must be nice. They always keep me here. Have you been to an institution?" I asked, assuming he knew the juvenile institution was where we would go after being sentenced.

"No."

"Do you think you're going to go to one this time?"

"Nope. I'm serving another month and then I'll get out of here. I can't wait."

"Are you still going to do burglaries?"

"Um, I don't know. Maybe I will and maybe I won't. Have you ever done a burglary?"

"Yeah, but it was a vacant house. I slept in it at night."

"So, you've never done a burglary for money?"

"Nope."

"Then you don't know how addictive it is."

"I guess not. Honestly, though, I don't think you should do them any longer. You've got a home with parents and siblings. They will miss you if you keep coming back here."

"Yeah. You're probably right."

"Where did you learn those exercises we've been doing?"

"My older brother was in the military and he showed me."

I was amazed at how hard it was to do the burpees and bear crawls. With burpees, you repeatedly alternate between doing push-ups and standing up. When you do them quickly and nonstop, they are taxing. Bear crawls consists of walking on your hands and feet and then doing push-ups at various intervals. Sprints were hard too, but I was familiar with running, so they weren't as taxing as the other two exercises.

I hung out with Dustin every time we came out of our cells. We were the minority in the pod; the African Americans were the majority. They basically controlled the TV. It was on BET at all times, which was fine. This didn't bother me because I stayed busy with my routine and with hanging out with Dustin. If we had spare time, we'd play cards. He taught me how to play spades; it took me a few days to fully grasp the game, but ultimately I learned how to play.

Once I was thoroughly versed on the rules of spades, Dustin wanted us to team up and gamble. I wasn't too enthused about this idea, but he eventually cajoled me into it.

"I don't have anything to gamble," I told him.

"That's fine. We'll gamble the food on our trays."

"I don't know, man."

"Come on. I need a partner. We aren't going to lose. It'll be like taking candy from a baby. The guys we'll play aren't that good."

"Who are we playing?" I asked amiably.

"Those two black guys," he said, pointing. One of them was big. He had cornrows and a weight lifter's physique. The other guy was shorter and skinnier. He looked like he was fifteen or sixteen years old, and he seemed to bounce when he walked. It was like he walked on his toes. I had played basketball with him before. His name was Ricky. For the most part, he seemed OK. The big guy's name was Tyrone. I didn't know him at all. Right off the bat, it was hard for me to adapt to the way they referred to us as honkies.

"Hey, Tyrone! Do you and Ricky want to play spades?" Dustin asked.

"Yeah! You two honkies want to get beat?" Tyrone said, speaking loudly and walking toward us.

"Shoot. You guys are going to lose," Dustin retorted.

"Well, put your money where your mouth is, white boy." Tyrone said.

"What do you want to gamble off of the tray?" Dustin asked. It was common for inmates to gamble food from their trays. We had no cash, change, or financial instruments like cash, coins, or credit cards. To make cards or games more interesting, we would gamble our various food items on our trays. In addition, the inmates maintained an underground barter system. The items would vary depending on price and availability. Normally, the barter system consisted of items bought from the commissary. We would trade these items for other items or services. For example, if someone ran out of coffee a few days before going to the store, he might trade some chips or candy for enough coffee to satisfy him until he went to the commissary. Sometimes, inmates bartered items for services, trading goods for haircuts, braids, or drawings. Inmates also traded contraband, such as drugs, pictures of naked girls, or tobacco.

"Let's bet the snack," Tyrone said, extending his hand to finalize the gamble.

"All right. Sounds good," Dustin agreed, shaking his hand.

"What about you, white boy," Tyrone asked.

"I'll gamble with Ricky," I said. For some reason, I didn't like Tyrone. Beyond the fact that he was big and loud, he also projected a shifty demeanor. I would have rather gambled with Ricky, since I knew him better. "Ricky. What do you want to shoot?"

"Let's shoot the fruit," Ricky responded quickly.

"Cool. Sounds good," I said, extending my hand to solidify

our bet. We all sat down at one of the metal tables that looked like a picnic table. Dustin shuffled the deck and dealt everyone a card facing up. When he flipped a jack in front of Ricky, he passed the cards to Ricky so that he could deal them. Ricky shuffled them again and then dealt them. The first few hands I got were great. They put us in the lead. After a few more hands, we had won the first game. It felt nice.

The next game was more neck and neck. It came down to ten points, but we handily beat them again. It felt really nice. At this point, I noticed a visible shift in the attitudes of our opponents. Tyrone was openly agitated. He picked up his cards roughly and scowled intensely when looking at them. After organizing them, he threw them down irately. This wasn't good. The next few hands did not calm him down. He seemed to get worse, grimacing and grunting at every other moment. He was clearly unhappy about the direction of the game. Dustin seemed to ignore him. Refusing to acknowledge Tyrone's tantrum, Dustin focused on organizing his cards. This caused Tyrone to huff and puff even more. Finally, he erupted and cussed as he threw the cards down.

"I quit!" he yelled and stalked off. Ricky looked perplexed. He didn't know if he should follow Tyrone or not. Eventually, he slowly slinked away to find Tyrone.

"This is going to get ugly, isn't it?" I asked Dustin.

"I don't know. Maybe it will. It depends on if he honors his bet or not. I'll let him calm down and then hit him up at dinner about the snack," Dustin said.

In a confined setting, it was a sign of weakness to accept disrespect. If the other inmates detected weakness, they would pounce. Instead of dealing with one instance of disrespect, you might then face multiple people disrespecting you. Therefore, it was advisable to handle disrespect immediately before it escalated. That was what Dustin planned to do. He couldn't allow Tyrone to not pay him, no matter how insignificant the snacks were. It was a matter of principle.

After a couple of hours, Dustin decided to confront Tyrone. He made sure to do so before dinner.

"Tyrone. You all right, man? You left pissed off," Dustin said cordially.

"You know why I was pissed off, white boy," Tyrone said gruffly.

"Unless you're mad about losing, I don't know," Dustin replied.

"Quit playing stupid. You cheated. I ain't paying nothing, honky," Tyrone said belligerently. According to prison etiquette, Dustin had only one option at this point. He had to fight Tyrone. He did not disappoint.

"Oh yeah? Then let's handle this in the cell," Dustin demanded, walking purposefully toward his cell. Tyrone dutifully followed him into the cell. We could hear the unmistakable sound of the two people rigorously fighting, wrestling, tussling, and scuffling. The whole pod was silent. The muted audience was riveted and focused intently on the closed cell door. I looked over at Ricky. We caught each other's eye at the same time. There was no hiding our sense of dread and trepidation. We were next. Ricky repeatedly looked at me and then at the closed cell door. He seemed to be unsure. He was not confident about what he should do. He looked baffled. I felt the same. What should we do? Ricky recovered from his befuddlement. Warily, he plodded down to his cell. I followed his movements with my eyes. I didn't know if I was supposed to follow him or not. Technically, Ricky had not disrespected me yet. That flimsy excuse became moot when Ricky waved me to his cell.

"Oh great. Here we go," I thought. Slowly, I ambled to his cell. He was waiting inside. Cautiously, I opened the door, stepped in, and locked the door behind me.

"Ricky, you know we didn't cheat. This is a stupid thing to fight over," I said somberly.

"If Tyrone said you did, then you did," Ricky said assuredly.

"I'm not paying either," He said. Later, I would question why I hadn't seen it before he had brandished it. He must have hidden it beside his thigh. There was no other explanation. When I saw the makeshift weapon, it made me pause. I was shocked. Surely, he did not plan on stabbing me. It was beyond my comprehension.

"Ricky put that..." I sputtered as he lunged at me. Reflexively, I extended my arms, opened my hands, and tried to block the first attempt. He swung the makeshift knife at my stomach, but he missed. Then he tried again. The next stab pierced my palm, impaling it. I managed to ignore the searing pain and close my hand around the knife. Tussling, we struggled for control over the weapon. I struggled valiantly, refusing to yield. I began kicking him vigorously, yet we persisted to grapple over the weapon. Finally, I bent it out of his grasp. At this point, we began wrestling. He pummeled my face vehemently. He was ruthless and unrelenting. I tried laboriously to return the blows.

He had the advantage. He had thrown the first punch, but I continued to strike him. Unfortunately, my blows were ineffectual. He had the upper hand. He was clearly winning. It felt like we were in combat for an hour. My blood was everywhere. I did not notice the cell door open. It wasn't until a staff member had jumped on us that I comprehended the implications. We had been caught. They must have heard us. Assertively, they attempted to peel us apart.

"Break it up!" the staff member yelled. I willingly released my grip on Ricky. I was ready for it to be over. I was completely drained. The staff member led me out of the pod and escorted me down the long hallway. Kids in different pods gawked at me. I kept my head up boldly. My bruised and bloody face testified to the brutal squabble. Words were not needed. I had gotten the worse end of it, but I refused to let them see any sign of weakness. I had to project rugged toughness, even though I was broken and dispirited inside. I was brought to the same seat that I had sat in when I had gotten beaten up during the programming session. The familiarity did not console me; there was no consoling me. I knew that I was in bad shape. I needed medical attention and the pain throbbing throughout my body evidenced that. The nurse ushered me into her medical room, which was the size of a closet. She told me to climb onto the examination table. Once I was situated, she began to probe and inspect my body.

"Let me see your right hand. It's bleeding all over the place," she complained.

"Sorry. I must have punctured it somehow," I lied. She did not believe me.

Nevertheless, she did not question me. She just dutifully swabbed, salved, and bandaged my wound. She did not, however, extricate the lead that was lodged deep in the palm of my hand. Ricky had made his weapon out of a sharp pencil. The broken lead is still visible to this day. It is a telling reminder that forces me to never forget the lesson that I learned that day.

I learned to never underestimate anyone. To this day, I diligently search for weapons before engaging in any skirmish. An otherwise benign instrument like a pencil, a toothbrush, a piece of metal, or a shaving razor can become a lethal weapon. I have seen inmates create some ingenious apparatuses. In addition to weapons, I have seen people make tools, utensils, and gadgets. When ordinary tools are banned, inmates create replacements. Some of my favorite gadgets are tattoo guns, salt lighters, remote controls, and liquor distilleries. Tattoo guns are expressly banned from all adult and juvenile prison facilities, yet inmates are heavily covered with tattoos. Inmates have perfected the art of making tattoo guns. They make them from a number of appliances, such as tape players, CD players, hard drives, beard trimmers, and typewriters. Basically, anything with a motor can be transformed into a tattoo gun. For tattoo needles, they use a variety of things, such as sewing needles, guitar strings, and metal brush bristles.

All that matters is they are made of metal and that they are the appropriate size. You sharpen the needle with a stone or a piece of concrete. Next, you attach it to the tattoo gun. There is no limit to the number of needles that you can attach. I've seen some tattoo guns with over ten needles. Needless to say, if the tattoo artist is decent, he can do some really good work. Even though it's legal in the free world, authorities uphold this ban because it's easy to transmit communicable diseases when tattoo artists are unsafe. That point is valid. Most of the time, though, the inmate who is getting tattooed will find his own needles, refusing to use anyone else's. I bet you are wondering what a salt lighter is. Well, it's a very creative way to produce fire. Smoking is banned in most state prison systems, so there are no matches or lighters. Of course, there's still a demand for lighters. Inmates need to light a number of things, including drugs, tobacco, tattoo ink, and food. The salt lighter is made with a toothbrush, paper clips, pencil lead, and a cup of salt water. The paper clips are fashioned into two separate prongs that are tied to the toothbrush. The prongs have three makeshift arms. One arm is configured to snugly hold the pencil lead between the separated paperclip on each side of the toothbrush. The other arm is fashioned to plug into an electrical socket. The last arm is bent downward. You do this with the paper clip on both sides of the toothbrush. Once you have configured the gadget, the last ingredient is a cup of salt water. You then plug the tool into a socket. Nothing will happen until you hold the cup of salt water under the two exposed arms that are bent downward. After you have followed all of the above instructions, the pencil lead will heat up and glow. If you touch anything to the cherry, you'll have a flame. It's that easy.

In most prisons, TV remote controls are banned. Don't ask me why but they are. To circumvent the hassle of getting up to turn the channel, inmates make contraptions to do this for them while they sit back on their bunks. They string lines along the wall that connect to their TVs. They tape broken pieces of white disposable Spork handles over the buttons on the TV and then connect these pieces to the strings. By pulling this string, they change the channels. It's pretty convenient, if you ask me. Liquor distilleries are just as innovative. Most inmates know how to make prison alcohol, which is also called pruno. Pruno is a crude form of wine. You can make this by combining sugar, yeast, and fermented fruit—or, in some cases, vegetables—together. The mixture will react and over a few days it will transform into pruno. The problem, however, is that it tastes bad and it takes a lot to get buzzed. In addition, it has been known to cause headaches, upset stomachs, and in some cases diarrhea. Needless to say, only die-hard alcoholics drink it on a regular basis. Pruno is not a total waste, though. You can convert it into hard liquor. It's not an easy process, but it can be done. You take the crude form of pruno and place it in a hot pot. You can buy these pots off commissary at most prisons to cook food or heat coffee. You will have to fiddle with the pot so that it can boil water. Usually, the manufacturer's setting barely gets the contents hot, and it's hard to get the water to boil. You then fashion some tubing into an airtight cover. Then you leave the pruno to boil. The steam vaporizes the liquor and pushes it up through the tubing. You place a bottle at the end of the tubing to collect the concentrated liquor. You repeat this process until you have made enough liquor. This liquor is potent.

After the nurse had examined me and bandaged me up, she gave me an ice pack and escorted me to the segregation pod at the end of the facility. I saw Dustin when I got there. He was standing at the door of his cell door. His swollen right eye was already starting to blacken, and he was smiling. Crusted blood surrounded his fat lip. The visible wounds contrasted greatly with his beaming countenance.

He smirked when I saw him. Tyrone and Ricky were also at their cell windows. Neither of them scowled at me or yelled any vulgar remarks. I also noticed that neither of them had visible wounds. They looked relatively untouched. I've come to realize that African Americans don't exhibit signs of fighting as visibly as white people. If I get tapped on my eye or nose, it will turn black and blue. Luckily for them, this isn't the case with African Americans. They escaped a lot of gawking. While we were in the segregation unit, though, Dustin and I maintained our rigorous workout schedules in our respective cells. We took birdbaths in our sinks when we were done. After a few days of being in segregation,

Ricky yelled over to me, "Daniel."

"Yep."

"Hey, thanks."

"For what?" I asked.

"For not telling about the pencil."

"It's all good, man."

"I really appreciate that. You could have destroyed my plans and my release date. So, thank you. If we end up in the same pod someday, I'll give you the fruit."

"Oh, thanks Ricky. Don't sweat the fruit though. It wasn't about that anyway. It was about the disrespect."

"Yeah, I'm sorry about that too."

It took a lot of courage for him to apologize to me. Normally, this wouldn't have happened. People never want to admit when they are wrong. Ricky had tacitly admitted that Tyrone had been wrong too. I doubt Tyrone liked that, but he didn't say anything.

CHAPTER 12

We were all sentenced to ten days in segregation. The first few days went by relatively quickly. My days there were filled with working out, reading, or talking to Dustin. I also found myself spending hours cleaning the cell. It was filthy when I had moved in. It had been filled with hair, mucus, boogers, toilet paper, and dry skin. I couldn't get comfortable in the cell until I cleaned it. I scrubbed it from ceiling to floor. Luckily, the staff members had no problem issuing the appropriate cleaning products. There was no way I was going to do a single push-up on that floor until I had scrubbed it.

I scrubbed it well, making it sparkling clean. After the first three days, it seemed like time was passing in slow motion. Every day was a drag. I tried to stay busy by keeping my mind occupied, but it was an arduous task that I failed at miserably. Nothing seemed to make my time go by more quickly. You can only do so much reading, working out and talking before everything becomes monotonous, dull, and drab. As you can imagine, this was especially hard for a kid to endure. Youngsters need to run around, socialize, and do stuff. Being confined takes a toll on a child.

This brings me to a common practice in the American judicial system: Administrative Segregation. Ad seg for short, is the practice of placing inmates in a cell for twenty three to twenty four hours a day. Apart from any other inmates. Solitary confinement was the old politically incorrect, way to say it. This seems to be the answer these days for just about any type of alleged misbehavior. I'm not talking about short stays. Increasingly, prisons and detention facilities are placing inmates into segregation for indefinite sentences. Depending on their individual prison sentences, inmates can be segregated for ten years or more. This is terrible. Can you picture an individual being released from prison after spending five to ten years in segregation? It's absolutely horrible for a person's mental health. I personally know people who have literally gone crazy from being in segregation. They often hear voices and talk to themselves. The reasons that prison officials place some inmates into indefinite segregation are remarkable. For example, California is the most active state with regard to incarcerating its citizens. The Department of Justice sued California to ease its overcrowded prison system; thankfully, they were mandated to release thousands of inmates. I can only imagine the inadequate medical facilities, sleeping arrangements, and hygiene facilities that they had. They were so overly burdened that they started housing inmates in gyms. It was ludicrous. At any rate, the prison administration in California is notorious for placing inmates on indefinite segregation. They will segregate certain inmates forever for simply being a member of a gang.

It is understandable that some people might agree with this situation, but I disagree. Allow me to provide a bare bones explanation of the membership processes of prison gangs. First off, prison is an artificial environment. Prisons were created to separate the inmates from society. This is fine, but the problem is that prisons house thousands of people at these facilities. Inmates have many different personalities and attitudes. They come from different backgrounds. There are bound to be differences, arguments, and confrontations. In an artificial environment like a prison, a person who is normally peaceful can be reduced to violence. In the outside world, if you don't have much in common with certain people, you naturally stay away from them. In prison, this is not an easy task. In prison, you are housed with many people you might not want to associate with. Getting away from them is not an option. The next logical step is to insulate yourself with people you feel comfortable with. In prison, people unsurprisingly divide themselves along racial lines. Is this because they are innately racist? No. First of all, all races act this way in prison.

Every race in the American prison system segregates itself from the others. People from different races don't hate each other, but they are most comfortable with members of their own race. If there is an argument or a problem within a race, the two parties can easily solve it. However, if members of two different races have an argument or a problem, it can quickly escalate into a full-fledged race war. How can you become comfortable when a powder keg like that is always ready to explode? You can't. Naturally, inmates segregate themselves according to race, and it is not hard to see how prison gangs were initially conceived. I am in no way justifying the existence of prison gangs. I am merely describing how they have thrived in this artificial environment. At the micro level, each race has their own individual gangs that police their own people. African Americans, for example, have Crips and Bloods. Hispanics have Surenos and Northenos. Whites have the Aryan Family and the Aryan Brotherhood. If one race did not have any gangs, the races that do have gangs would prey on them. America has a military to protect itself, and these races similarly have gangs to protect themselves. Of course, gangs are also involved in negative activities, including violence, crime, and predatory actions. I'm not excusing any of that, but some aspects are positive. For example, most gangs require their members to work out daily, read books, avoid television, and write essays. It is unfair to make blanket judgments on all gangs. All gang members should be allowed to determine their own direction. If gang members are determined to act predatory, violent, or criminal, then judge them by this.

However, this is exactly what California and many other states do. They place gang members as a whole on indefinite administrative segregation for simply being in a gang. That is just a convenient way out to deal with groups of people you don't understand. This kind of approach harkens back to previous eras of backward thinking. If the practice of administrative segregation were limited to harmful acts, then that would be fine. However, this is not the case. Increasingly, prison systems are building and maintaining facilities for one purpose: administrative segregation. In my opinion, this is injurious. It causes inmates to become mentally disturbed.

It might be hard for mainstream America to digest this, but somebody needs to analyze the benefits and drawbacks of this type of punishment. It's surprising to me that this controversial issue isn't drawing more attention in the field of psychology. We need to focus on this before too many inmates lose their sanity.

The time that I spent in segregation went so slowly that Dustin and I had to engineer things to do. We settled on chess because it was a game that we both knew how to play. Since we were not allowed to leave our cells or use chessboards, we had to make our own board and pieces. I made a board out of a regular piece of paper, measuring the squares and formatting them to fit on the page. Then I made the pieces. Some inmates like to get creative and make them out of toilet paper or wet paper. I, however, was not that creative. I simply cut little square pieces of paper and wrote the initials of the chess figures on them. That was it. It was nothing spectacular.

With our newly configured chessboard, we numbered each square so that we could call out our moves to each other. On each game, we would gamble push-ups to make it interesting. Dustin won the majority of the games, so I ended up with a good workout. My chest was pumped up. I needed all the exercise that I could get, since my nightmares continually kept me from sleeping. Every time I closed my eyes and fell asleep, I'd be transported to that dreaded alleyway. I found that the best way to escape my nightmares was to wear myself out. If I was exhausted and didn't have the energy to dream, then I would escape them. The problem, however, was that I had to work out for hours to be this fatigued. It was hard to do. If I didn't do this, my nightmares would keep me sleepless and I would constantly wake up sweating and out of breath. It was horrible.

CHAPTER 13

—◦◦◦◦—

M r. Simms," a tiny voice squawked over the intercom in my cell. "Get ready. Staff is coming to bring you to court."

"OK. I'm ready," I told her. It was a little past eight o'clock in the morning. I had been up for a few hours. I couldn't sleep again because of the nightmares. I had been in the hole for nine long days. The next day was my last day in segregation, so I was happy.

I wondered which pod they were going to take me to. I hated entering new pods. It was always such a disturbing moment. Everyone in the pod would look at you and size you up. I hated how hostile they would be. Why couldn't they just smile and welcome me into the fold when I walked in? That would have been nice, but it was wishful thinking. In juvenile detention, the African American gangsters got the warmest welcome. Their buddies would slap them on the back, laugh, and ask what they were in for. They would ask if they needed some bars of soap, coffee, or food. They would give them a phone to call their friends or family. They would give them whatever they needed.

When I walked into a new pod with my arms around my bedroll, everyone in the whole pod would get silent and watch me carefully. It was like they were waiting to see if anyone would speak up and claim me as a friend. No one ever did. I would quietly walk over to the staff desk and meekly ask what cell I was in. They'd tell me where to go and I would slink past all of the unfriendly faces. I would make sure to smile broadly to all of the other kids, but they would meet my smile with menacing and threatening looks. Occasionally, a bigger and tougher kid would slam his shoulder against me and tell me to watch where I was going. I'd act like it had been my fault and apologize. I would then continue to my new cell. If I had a hostile cellmate, he'd tell me I had to find a different cell. I'd have to walk among the mugging faces until I found the rare kid who would look beyond my skin color. I'd ask him if I could move in with him. If he agreed, I'd have to ask the staff to move me. I would have to make up some lame excuse about why I couldn't move into the cell he had initially assigned me. It was hell.

The prejudice that I faced never failed to amaze me. I can honestly say that I wasn't racist in the least, yet the other kids immediately treated me like a pariah because of my skin color. I was a honky and they couldn't look beyond that. No matter how hard I tried to endear myself to them, they'd just clown me and put me down. I found that my best approach was to act indifferent. I would simply not talk to anyone. I would let the friendly faces gravitate toward me unbidden.

All other approaches failed miserably. The loud crack of the cell door being unlocked made my stomach lurch. I pushed the door open and stepped in. "I hope I get some good news at court," I thought. I still had not met my attorney. Getting an attorney was always a crapshoot. Would I get one who zealously defended my rights, or one who just wanted to shove a plea bargain down my throat? The majority of them were interested in getting a plea bargain. My case would have been great for zealous attorneys. It would have given them the opportunity to scrutinize the evidence and catch something that the police had missed. They would have seen that an adult had pressured me to claim that I had stolen the car. This kind of thing rarely happened, though. Instead, the court-appointed attorney would hurriedly terrorize the defendant by telling them about all of the evidence that was stacked against them. The attorney would say that the defendant had no chance in a trial. The attorney would say that the defendant should plead guilty and that any other move would be foolhardy. The attorney would file no motions or affidavits.

Their sole purpose was to force feed whatever plea bargain the prosecutor had offered in his infinite knowledge. Beyond this, there wasn't much hope for a defense. Additionally, cases were often sabotaged. Public defenders get livid if you refuse a plea bargain. It is no secret that the wheels of "just-us" would falter if the sheeple revolted and refused to plea bargain. They wouldn't know what to do if that happened. Regrettably, however, indigent defendants such as myself would suffer the most. The reason the justice system would falter is because courts do not have the capacity to prosecute everyone they charge. Charging someone with a crime with the intent of taking them to trial is rare. In most cases the prosecutor will charge as many crimes possible, even if some of the crimes are different from the underlining offense, in the hopes the offender will plead guilty to some lesser offense. There was a running joke amongst inmates that you could come to jail for jaywalking, but end up charged for manslaughter. The point being, they charged crimes that didn't happen, so you'll be inclined to plead to what did happen. A prime example, is, the guy who shoplifts at a store ends up charged for robbery. This happens more than you might think. If all these over charged inmates actually went to trial, the courts would be forced to let many go. They simply do not have enough court rooms and court personnel to handle every individual they charge. And even if they tried to accomplish it, indigent defendants with Public Defenders would be pushed through inadequate trials to make way for the more moneyed inmates. There is a clear disparagement between defendants with money and those without. But that goes for everything, it is the lifeblood of a free-market. You get what you pay for, and if you can't pay for counsel you are in trouble.

"Mr. Simms, where are you?" a bespectacled older man yelled. He was wearing a wool dress coat with patches on the elbows.

"Over here," I replied. I was in a small cell outside of the waiting area of the courtroom. With purpose, the gentleman sauntered over to the front of my cell. He pulled a file out of a worn brown leather briefcase and opened it.

"How are you, Mr. Simms?"

"Nervous."

"That's to be expected. You're in for taking a motor vehicle without permission. That's a Class C felony. From what I gather, you confessed to the crime. Is that correct?"

"Um. Yes, sir. So, you are my attorney? What is your name?" I asked.

"I'm sorry. Yes, I'm your attorney. I'll be representing you. My name is Mr. Brewster."

"Nice to meet you," I told him.

I couldn't help but look at his disheveled appearance. His hair was windblown, messy, and unkempt. A two-day beard adorned his face. Specks of some white substance blotched the lenses of his glasses. It was possibly milk or some other foreign substance I'd rather not dwell on. He was wearing corduroy trousers and penny loafers. Luckily, there were no pennies in them. I didn't want to judge a book by its cover, though. He could be an astute scholar of the law. He could be brilliant at poking holes in cases. He could be good at discerning what was right or wrong for his clients. He could be quick-witted. I hoped that he was all of these things.

"Well, Mr. Simms, there's not much for you to do in this case other than plead guilty. I can get a lenient sentence for you and then send you on your way," he said. He chuckled at his witticism, but I did not laugh.

"Send me on my way? With how much time?" I asked sternly.

"Well, you are looking at a few months."

"That's the best you can get me?"

"Yep. Unless there are any mitigating circumstances."

"Mitigating circumstances? What does that mean?"

"It refers to reasons why you shouldn't get the maximum due to extenuating factors," he said.

"I still don't understand."

"Oh, don't worry about it. There are no mitigating factors in this case," he stated perfunctorily.

"All right. I have a question, though. Are there any programs that can help me once I'm done with this sentence?"

"Programs? Yes, you'll get probation."

"I'm not talking about probation. I need assistance to get off of the streets. I'm homeless."

"Oh, um, I don't know. I'll look into it. What we're going to do today is called the arraignment. After being read the charges, you will enter your plea. You will plead not guilty. Any questions?"

"Nope."

"OK. Good. Other than entering not guilty, let me do all of the talking."

"All right."

"See you inside in about ten minutes," he stated, sliding his loafers around and gliding toward the waiting room.

"Mr. Simms," yelled a tired, droopy-eyed staff member.

"Over here," I said, notifying her of my presence.

"You are up," she said, unlocking my cell with a big brass key. "Follow me."

"OK," I acquiesced, following her obediently. She led me through the waiting room of the court. As I passed many bystanders and patrons, they curiously leered back at me. Along with my tan sandals, my dark-blue canvas top and bottom instantly identified me as a delinquent.

Finally, we wound ourselves through the waiting room and arrived at a door. The staff member then ushered me in through the door. The wood-paneled room had two grandiose oak tables. My attorney, Mr. Brewster, was sitting at one of them, and the fresh-faced prosecutor sat at the other one. The judge's wooden platform was empty.

My attorney waved me over. "Hey. I talked to the prosecutor," he whispered conspiratorially. "He'll let you plead as charged," he said with a straight face, as if it were a privilege to plead guilty. This definitely wasn't the discerning advocate I had craved.

"As charged? That doesn't sound like a deal to me," I replied.

"Well, you confessed to the crime," he razzed.

"Whatever. How much time is he trying to give me?"

"Around five months."

"What about getting help when I get out?" I asked.

"I looked into that. There is nothing," he said.

"That's crazy. So, I'm going to be released with the shirt on my back and that's it?"

"Yep, I guess so. Your probation officer might be able to help you somehow."

"No. I've already asked him."

"Then I don't know."

"Great. Well, I've got to think about that plea bargain. It doesn't sound too much like a deal, but I'll think about it."

"Don't take too long to decide. He might pull it."

"Pull it? And then what would happen?"

"You'd have to go to trial."

"How do you pull a plea if it's a plea to the charges?" I asked.

"He'll pull his recommendation and go for the maximum. Five months is in the middle of the range."

"Can you negotiate for the low end?"

"No. They're not budging off of the midrange recommendation."

"OK. Whether or not we got to trial, I'll be facing the same charge? I'll have to think about this."

"If you go to trial, the court will find you guilty for sure."

"Why do you say that?"

"Because it'll be a judge trial."

"A judge trial? How come I can't have a jury trial?"

"They're not offered in juvenile court."

I still find this remarkable. There are no jury trials for juveniles. How ridiculous is that? Even my overworked attorney in the penny loafers perceived the inherent prejudice in this situation.

"You'll get found guilty for sure," he said. They were treating me just like every other kid who went through there. I was guilty of participating in the theft of a car, yet not all kids are guilty. What about innocent kids? Don't they deserve a jury trial? This seems unfair.

"All arise," the court reporter bellowed. "The Honorable McKinnely presiding." Everyone in the room stood up.

"You may be seated," the judge stated. "For the record, the parties present are convened for case number 94-36321-41, taking a motor vehicle without permission. Mr. Simms, have you conferred with your attorney?"

"Yes."

"Did he discuss the charges with you?"

"Yes."

"OK. To the charge of taking a motor vehicle without permission, how do you plead?"

"Not guilty," I replied with butterflies in my stomach.

"Do you understand the charges?"

"Um, I think so."

"OK. That's a yes, correct?"

"Correct."

"All right. I'll accept your plea. I am binding the case over for trial. The next hearing will be on February 6th. Thank you," he said apathetically. "Court dismissed."

That was it. All of my anxiousness had built up to this brief moment. The more I entered courtrooms, the more desensitized I got. I guess the same could be said for committing crimes. Regrettably, I quickly got desensitized to them. The tired, droopy-eyed staff member ushered me out of the courtroom and back down to the holding cell. From the holding cell, a staff member escorted me back to my bleak cell in segregation.

The whole process took two and a half hours. I made it back in time for lunch of peanut butter and jelly sandwiches.

"What happened?" Dustin asked curiously.

"Nothing. I just plead not guilty."

"Did they offer you a plea bargain?"

"Yeah, but it wasn't a bargain. They want me to plead as charged."

"What? That's weak. They'll offer something better in the future."

"I don't know. My attorney sounded pretty adamant."

"They always do."

"It sucks that they don't have any help for me when I get out of here. I asked my attorney about it. He said there was nothing."

"Yeah, that does suck."

"You're lucky. When you get out, you can go home. I don't have anywhere to go. I'll probably be back here within weeks."

"Yeah. That is messed up, dude. Well, if you had money you could buy your own place."

"I don't have money!"

"You can make it easily. Do what I do: burglaries."

"I don't know, man."

"You'll have more money than you'll know what to do with."

"Burglaries scare me. When I broke into the vacant house, it was different. That place was empty. No one was lurking around to blow my head off."

"Nah. You shouldn't be scared, bro. They're easy. All you have to do is scope the garage or the parking spaces of a house. If there's no car, go and knock. Pound on the door or ring the doorbell a bunch of times. If no one answers, go around the periphery until you find a way in. Once you get in, go to the master bedroom and start collecting the loot: jewelry, cash, guns, video cameras, or whatever you can find. Every house has something of value."

"You make it sound easy. What if someone is hiding or arrives while you're in there?"

"You run like hell," he said, laughing.

"Hmm."

My criminal barometer ticked up a notch. He had piqued my interest. Since I would be forced to leave the juvenile detention facility without anything, it was an attractive option. Unfortunately, it was maybe the only way for me to feasibly overcome my homelessness.

CHAPTER 14

O ver here," I yelped, running down the basketball court. "I'm open. I'm open."

    I had been out of segregation for a couple of weeks. I had moved to a new pod. Dustin and I were split up. The pod I was in now was relatively mellow. I received the normal hard looks when I arrived, but they thankfully faded swiftly. I had gotten chummy with an Asian guy named Tony and two African Americans named Dante and Anthony.

    Dante had asked me to play basketball on his team. Intent on playing, I stood along the wall with eight other kids. Normally, they would pick all of the African Americans first and then either pick me last or not at all. Luckily, the team captain was Dante. He picked me third, which was a boost to my low self-esteem. I was beaming.

    I met Dante after I had sat at his table for chow. Tony and Anthony were sitting there too. We had committed the same crime, and this initially bridged the gap between us. He was in for car theft too. The only difference was that he had stolen cars to take on joyrides. I didn't agree with what he had done, but I didn't allow this to dim my prospects of making a friend. I needed all of the friends I could get. As a honky, I was not exactly a popular cohort.

It's interesting to look back at the early nineties and the midnineties. It was a very confusing point in time for many white kids, including me. It seemed like it was cool to be African American at that time. Rap was reaching a pivotal moment. Movies like *Menace to Society* and *Boyz n the Hood* glorified the urban gangster lifestyle, while movies like *White Men Can't Jump* disparaged white people, portraying them as the nerdy, weak, out-of-touch, and spineless. All of this contributed greatly to a cultural identity crisis. It was common to see white guys braiding their hair in cornrows, sagging their pants, and claiming to be members of black gangs. The tough and cool characters they wanted to emulate were all black. It wasn't until the early 2000's that Eminem, a commercially acceptable white guy, was able to break into the rap game. Vanilla Ice had also been successful, but I view him as more of a passing fad than a genuine artist. Today, however, there are a variety of white rap artists. One in particular, Macklemore, grew up right down the street from me. I am happy for his success. My point, though, is that it was a trying climate to grow up in, and it added greatly to the pressure of being white and incarcerated. It was common for inmates to test or ridicule the white boy. This was incredibly brutal, difficult, and demanding. I was forced to become tough and to protect myself from the constant barrage of attacks. The moment that kid has thrashed me while I was trapped in that desk, I discovered this fact. Incidents like the fiasco with the spade game reinforced this reality. The dirty looks, the derogatory words, and the ostracism made things hard for me, but the constant adversity fortified me. I didn't even realize it. I didn't know that one day all of those experiences would turn me into a strong, articulate, and self-possessed individual. I'm not tough like a thug. Instead, my toughness goes unexpressed. Ironically, my appearance was not exactly the kind of characteristic that would help me thrive in such a vicious environment. I was often targeted because of my looks. I resented the negative attention that I had received from inmates and from the priest and John because of my looks.

"You've got a good hook and lay-up," Dante complimented me after we had won the game. "But you've got to work on your dribbling skills."

"Yeah, I know. I've always been dreadful at it," I said."

You'll get better. One problem is that you incessantly eye the ball while you're dribbling. Don't do that. You're using it as a crutch, and it will keep you from getting better. You need to focus on running, turning, bending, and maneuvering the dribbling ball without looking at it."

"If I do that, I might get the ball swatted out of my hand."

"Eventually, though, the ball will be an extension of your arm and you'll be able to keep it from being taken from you."

"All right, Dante. Thanks for the input. I'll work on it."

"Good. Your game will be elevated if you do." Dante was a couple of years older than me, so he was a kind of big brother to me. This was fine with me. I needed guidance for more things than basketball. I found myself starving for it. Ultimately, however, I reached a point of self-reliance.

Something bothered me about Dante, though. His poise would change depending on the company he kept. Around me he talked and acted one way, but around his black counterparts he'd revert to slang and jiving. I didn't like that. I just wanted to scream, "Be yourself!" His demeanor just reeked of fakeness.

In his defense, however, in that time and place it must have been hard to maintain a tough facade while associating with a fourteen-year-old white kid.

It was impossible to find someone I could get comfortable enough to talk candidly with. All of the other kids were trying so hard to project their toughness. The racial differences were also extremely hard to overcome. For instance, Anthony and I had a brief contentious discussion over the word *boy*. Anthony was about one year older than me. He seemed to be fairly level-headed. He carried himself well, but I noticed that he was overly attentive to whatever I said. He didn't exactly detract from what I said, nor was he particularly congenial. He would look for hidden meanings and make obscure connections with what I said. It was like he was expecting to discover that I was an undercover racist. That hurt me. I truly did not care about his race, but he seemed to think I did. His suspicions caused him to confront me about calling him boy. I had said it in jest while we were in the midst of cheery banter.

I said, "Come on, boy. Quit lying." He pulled me aside and got in my face. I hadn't even seen it coming. He was pissed. He told me that I was using it in a racial and derogatory manner. He couldn't have been further from the truth. I apologized for him taking it the wrong way. He explained there were historically racial connotations with the word *boy*. How could I have known that? We almost fought and I didn't have a clue about the significance of our conflict. This caused me to focus intently on being cautious. I didn't want to accidentally say the wrong thing. This situation also distanced me from him. I couldn't risk offending him.

CHAPTER 15

There is no easy way to accurately describe the sense of hopelessness that began to set in. The negative and hostile atmosphere of the juvenile detention facility had taken its toll. I felt no love, joy, or compassion. It all began to suffocate me. I had no outlet. I had no shoulder to cry or lean on. I had no support. Instead, I had to learn to be more self-reliant.

This was hard. It was almost impossible. I genuinely wanted to just be a fourteen-year-old kid. It was especially troubling to be confronted with the cold reality of my life. I really needed someone to talk to. I needed anyone, but no one was there for me. The staff members maintained an air of indifference and cool inaccessibility. They did not invite anyone to confide in them. Instead, they projected unapproachability. What is that all about? I was slowly slipping back into the practice of ignoring and suppressing my pain. I needed to express my true feelings, but instead I was smothering them. The way I looked at it, there was no way I could share my feelings with any of the other kids. With them, I had to maintain a hard exterior. Otherwise, they would exploit my weaknesses in some way.

As I woke up each morning in juvie, I would look around with a jaundiced eye at the various methods of control, restraint, and captivity. Everything was so sanitary and cold. I saw no vestiges of a society that wanted me to succeed, turn my life around, or become a so-called productive member of society. People would say that they wanted to help, but nobody had an actual strategy to help inmates become productive member of society.

To keep myself from falling into the negativity that was surrounding me, I spent all my free time voraciously reading. When I was reading, I got to escape my dismal environment. I was transported to settings that I would daydream about. Writers like Sidney Sheldon, Michael Connelly, and John Grisham became my friends. Juvie was such a fluid and transient setting. I couldn't develop genuine relationships there. I called them friends, but were they really "friends." Like me, they were being held captive. How could we maintain genuine friendships in such an adverse setting?

I read every book I could get my hands on. I would get lost in the plot, the characters, and the story line. My reading skills were terrible. I struggled through each story. Reading one book would take me weeks. I slogged through them, though. My sixth-grade reading level was enough to drive me through each page. Sometimes I would stop on a word, ponder it, and then find the definition. I would then write a sentence with the word.

That was my school. I was unable to satisfy my insatiable appetite. I longed for the days when I had received a proper education. My self-driven education, however, was better than nothing. I enjoyed it. I savored every moment of it. Being enabled to flee my captors was priceless, invaluable, and necessary. When I was lost in a plot, I would forget about my pain, my family, and my incarceration. The stories would temporarily hold them in abeyance. Sometimes I would tell myself that I didn't need anything except for my books.

Books were my family, my friends, and my source of freedom. They were everything to me. Miraculously, they even kept me from thinking about Tammie. Whenever I would set down a book, however, thoughts would swirl up and demand my attention. I couldn't believe that Tammie wasn't writing to me. I hadn't received any answers from her. My letters were not coming back, which meant that she was getting them. What could be the problem? I worried about her so much. My longings were tangible. I felt my heartstrings being pulled to and fro. I couldn't do anything, though, but pine over her.

My heartsickness grew worse when I pondered my future. What was I going to do when I got out? Where would I sleep and shower? What would I eat? All of these issues needed my attention. I continued to put off thinking about them. I had to do better than sleeping in stolen cars when I got out. I hated doing that. I would always have to sleep with one eye open. I would have to have all of my clothes on. I would have to be ready to run if a savvy cop stumbled upon me. Forget that. I wanted a home. I needed to discover a better way to somehow reach my goal.

CHAPTER 16

"All arise," the court reporter boomed. "The Honorable Charles McKinnely presiding."

As I stood up, I looked around at the other folks in the room. I was early. Another hearing was underway. A kid I didn't know was being arraigned for assault. The kid had his street clothes on, which meant that he was free. I was envious.

My desire to be free grew stronger when I saw him. Even though freedom had its own set of dangers, it was better than being locked up like an animal. I looked at the kid's dad, mom, and siblings. His dad wore a suit and his mom wore a business suit. Clearly, they were important people in their respective fields. Was it wrong for me to want to join their family? Was this a treasonous thought against my own family? If it was, I was guilty. I watched the dad's gestures. He had one arm around his two toddlers, and he gave his wayward son a reassuring squeeze with his other hand. As his son walked up to the defendant's table, he looked back at his dad. His father nodded and smiled at him encouragingly. His dad held his mother's hand. As they were holding hands, I could see the tension in their taunt white knuckles. He was in torment. I ached for that kind of love. The father felt immense distress for his child. I could almost feel their agony. I would have done anything for this connection. I would never feel this kind of compassion, though. There was no one in the courtroom for me. If I were sentenced harshly, no one would care but me. This hurt immensely. It caused me to reexamine the painful truth that I had discovered at the age of ten. On the porch of my first foster home, I was alone as I tried hopelessly to find my way. The absence of my family was especially poignant. When I saw cohesive family units, the strong bonds that tied them together made me incredibly self-conscious. To this day, seeing a loving family makes me yearn to be part of a family. How pitiful is that? I loathed the reality of it, but I couldn't do anything to change my situation. I longed to have my family back, but it was out of my hands.

The kid's arraignment went by quickly. He pleaded not guilty. A high-priced attorney sat next to him. The attorney took command of the courtroom. He detailed the motions, memorandums, and affidavits that had been filed in the case. He seemed to captivate the judge and the staff members in the court. His expensive cufflinks were shiny. Then he was done talking. After this hearing, my shabby attorney sauntered up to the defendant's table and set down his brown leather briefcase. It appeared especially ratty and worn compared to the other attorney's briefcase. He clumsily pulled my file out, bending the corners of it.

He was wearing the same tacky coat with the patches on the elbows. The same penny loafers adorned his feet. Thankfully, he had changed his pants. He had replaced the corduroys with a pair of tan slacks. A drop of coffee was on them. He was a far cry from the other attorney. He had no stage presence at all. He was a nonentity. He was a minion. The judge talked to him like an exasperated elder, cutting him off repeatedly. It was painful to watch.

The situation was especially troubling to me. I was pleading guilty. A week before my hearing on February 6th, I had called my attorney to tell him about my decision. I had also called him a few times before that. In each call, he reiterated the benefits of pleading guilty. I didn't have much faith in getting a better deal. For good reason, Mr. Brewster did not intend to bargain further. He thought that there would not be a better plea, but he had arrived at this conclusion without first discussing it with the prosecutor. It was based on his experiences with past cases. He told me, "It is a very good deal." He said that it was a deal that wouldn't get better.

Needless to say, I reluctantly pleaded guilty. I was not confident in the case, my attorney, the judge, or the judiciary. Therefore, I felt that this was the only option. It would have been nice to have someone to discuss my options with. The only person I had was my attorney, and he was pushing the plea down my throat. There was nothing neutral about his position. He wanted to keep the cases churning. He wanted to reduce his caseload.

"Hello, Mr. Simms. We're convened today to discuss your sentencing in Case No. 94-36321-41, taking a motor vehicle without permission," Judge Charles McKinnely said. "Did anyone offer you any promises to plead guilty?"

"No," I said, as my voice cracked. My pubescence and nerves combined to discompose me.

"Did anyone threaten, coerce, or cause you duress to plead guilty?"

"No."

"Is this plea made knowingly, willingly, and intelligently?"

"Um, yes," I croaked.

"OK, I'll rule that you have voluntarily entered into this plea. What is the prosecutor's recommendation?"

"Twenty-two weeks, Your Honor," the fresh-faced prosecutor said. "Does the defense agree with this recommendation?"

"Yes, Your Honor."

"All right. I'll go with the prosecutor's recommendation. I am sentencing you to twenty-two weeks. Your sentence will be served in the Washington State Juvenile Institutional System. You are also receiving twelve months of probation. When you are released, you are to report to your probation officer. Do you understand?"

"Yes," I said.

"OK. Do you have any more questions, Mr. Simms?"

"Uh. Yes, Your Honor. I do."

"OK. What is it?" he said perfunctorily. He was clearly hoping to keep the cases moving. His impatience was visible. Why had he asked if I had any questions? My attorney shot me a perturbed look. He didn't want me to talk unless I was answering questions.

"I have been asking my attorney for any resources or programs to help me get off of the streets. I'm homeless. Do you know of any?"

"I can't say I do, Mr. Simms. What we do here involves criminal cases. We don't deal with welfare. Now, if you don't have any questions regarding your criminal case, then we're done here," he said irritably.

"No, Your Honor. I have no more questions," I said sheepishly, averting my eyes and dropping my head to my chest.

I had ceased being a child long before this exchange, but I was astonished at how they treated me. I wondered if they treated the adolescent kids who mowed their lawns the same way. It was immensely hard for me to gather the courage to reach out for help, yet they had dismissed me like I was a nuisance, a pest, or a headache. I hated that. I resented them for being jerks.

CHAPTER 17

———◇○◦⌒◦○◇———

Y ou're not going to move in there, are you?" a random inmate asked. I had just been transferred to Naisell Youth Center. The same nondescript suburban SUV had transported me. I savored the scenery as we drove. The facility was close to the border of Washington and Oregon. The compound was laid out in a semicircular fashion. Each unit had a walkway that led to a communal chow hall. There was an education building and a recreational building. The facility was in the middle of nothingness. There were no trees, towns, or commercial businesses in sight. What set the facility apart from others was that it did not have a perimeter fence. There was nothing to stop the kids from escaping. This seemed to indicate that there was an honor system. Surprisingly, it worked; no one escaped while I was there.

As soon as I arrived, I was issued bedding, clothing, and indigent hygiene supplies. I was directed to a specific cell. As I was walking past the hostile foreign faces, a couple of kids approached me.

"A rapist lives in that cell," a tall, pimply kid said.

"Great," I thought. "Just what I need: prison politics."

It never failed to amaze me how people would differentiate, create divisions, and build hierarchies. This kind of behavior naturally exists below the conscious level. It is primal.

At one point, our instincts were essential to survive. We were forced to create clans, tribes, and bands of people to combat the dangers of the world. In these clans, tribes, and bands, certain people would naturally enter into positions of leadership. These people would explicitly or implicitly be the main authority figures. To this day, our inherited instincts reign. Our need for authority has led to the establishment of governments, organizations, and religions. The pervasive influence of these establishments is inescapable. It is not hard to see why inmates created divisions. Including myself, most inmates are not sexually deviant. Contrary to rampant misconceptions, most inmates don't beat, rape or kill women and children. In reality, most inmates shun and ostracize that type of offender.

Whether this tendency is positive or negative, it happens at most confinement facilities, and I wasn't planning on bucking the trend.

"Oh yeah? Forget that. I ain't moving in there," I said, feigning toughness. "Are any cells open with someone solid?"

When an inmate had been incarcerated for a crime that wasn't maligned, we would say that he was solid or that he had a solid beef.

"Um, I think his cell is open," the pimply kid said, pointing at a different kid.

"My name is Jason. Nice to meet you," the kid said. I had passed their test. I had overcome the rapist barometer.

"Nice to meet you too," I said, extending my hand. "My name is Daniel."

"Go over and introduce yourself to Gary. He'll probably let you move in with him."

"All right. Thanks," I said, walking over to Gary. "Hey. How's it going? My name is Daniel." I told him, extending my hand.

"Nice to meet you."

Gary was a short, barrel-chested kid. He was probably a couple of years older than me. His face was round and affable. He had a good-natured disposition.

"I hear your cell is open. Is that true?"

"Yep. You want to move in?"

"Yeah. Is that OK with you?"

"Yes, that's fine. I need a cellmate. Do you snore?"

"No."

"You'll have the top bunk. Do you have a problem cleaning? I clean every other day. If you move in, we'll take turns. Is that OK with you?"

"No problem. I'm a clean person."

"Cool."

"Do you know who I have to talk to?"

"Go and talk to her," he said, pointing at a middle-aged woman. "She's cool."

"All right. Thanks," I said, ambling over to the round, barrier-type counter, that separated her from the milling juveniles, she was sitting in a swivel office chair that allowed her to observe the dayroom from all angles. "Hello. I just got here today and I need your help."

"With what?" she replied responsively.

"I would like to move in with Gary," I said, pointing Gary out to her.

"Oh yeah? The normal protocol is for you to submit a move slip. The moves are done once a week."

"That won't work in this situation."

"Oh yeah? Why not?" she said, perking up.

"The cell I was assigned to houses a guy I have problems with. To avoid further issues, I'd like to move in with Gary. I know him. We'll get along better," I said, slightly misleading her.

"Where do you know the guy you have problems with?"

"King County Juvenile," I said deceitfully.

"All right. Go ahead and move your stuff into Gary's cell. I'll go and change your cell assignment."

"Thank you."

"You're welcome," she said, smiling.

By following the protocol, the inmates immediately accepted me into the inner sanctum of solid inmates. It was not like this was some herculean feat. I had a solid beef. My crime ensured my admittance. This is pathetic. The validation process should be more stringent. It should be based on character, integrity, honor, and steadfastness.

In defense, however, the initial validation process was just the first peg. It provided the key to get through the door. Your acceptance depended on your social skills, your toughness, and your grit. You couldn't be soft, weak, or spineless. These traits weren't admirable in the confined setting of prison. Most inmates strive to be big and tough. They work out all of the time. This is the stereotypical prisoner cliché. I was an oddity, though. I followed my own tune, but I didn't buck the prison norms. For instance, I worked out daily, engaged in social banter, and fought if someone disrespected me. Instead of playing cards, watching TV, or otherwise wasting my time, though, I read on my spare time. This was irregular among my peers. They would only read if all other avenues of entertainment were unavailable.

Looking back, I realize that reading was my coping mechanism. I wasn't just escaping the harsh realities of my incarceration; I was escaping my life completely. I hated my life, so I found the next best thing. I lost myself in the lives of the characters in the books I read. It was a very sad situation.

CHAPTER 18

When I was a kid, time seemed to go by at a snail's pace. The same was true of my incarceration. Minutes seemed like hours. Days were like weeks. It was horrible. Nothing I did managed to alleviate the agony.

I filled every day doing as much as I could. Regrettably, my options were severely limited. I would wake up, freshen up, and eat breakfast. Between breakfast and lunch, I would read. After lunch, I would go to the recreation area and work out. We all had to return to our cells at four o'clock so that the staff members could take attendance. They had to make sure no one had escaped. During the count, I would read. Dinner came next and then the night was practically over. We had no more activities after that. It was extremely drab, dreary, and monotonous. The routine never strayed. There was no variation.

Occasionally, some spontaneous action might occur. For instance, some inmates had a loud argument over a card game. It cooled down, though, and did not escalate. Other than that particular argument, it was surprisingly relatively calm. One thing I was not able to do, though, was go to school. This was troubling. They said I didn't have enough time. How stupid was that? Having a five-month sentence meant that I couldn't participate in any educational pursuits. The whole time I was there, I didn't go to school once.

I was basically left to my own devices. This was not very helpful. My thoughts invariably reverted back to my family. Where were they? Were they OK? In moments of introspection, I found myself questioning the past. Why had my parents abandoned me in the first place? What had I done to deserve this? It hurt me to think about this, but I wanted to grasp it. I couldn't shake the need to know. I was determined to find out someday. I was determined to confront my parents one at a time and uncover the truth. This would not alter anything. The damage was irreversible, but I needed to know about their reasons. From the depths of my soul, I had to make sense of it. I promised myself that someday I would travel to Tennessee to find out why my father had left me. It was important for me to do this. I couldn't allow the distance to interfere with my objective. To end my heartbreak, I needed closure.

I was also perplexed about why Tammie hadn't written to me. It drove me crazy, but there was nothing I could do about it. I tried to forget her. I was debating whether to break up with her if she had no valid reason for not writing to me. Without sending me a memo, she might have just ended things and moved on without telling me. This possibility stung but I had to accept it. If being abandoned taught me anything, I learned to expect the unexpected. I learned to not trust anyone. I learned to never get too attached. Attachments would only end up hurting me again. That was unacceptable.

I was destined to live in a world of loneliness. Eventually, my time slowly inched by. No matter how thrilled I was to get out, I was incredibly apprehensive. How could I not be? I had no idea about what I was going to do about shelter, food, or my future. All of the planning in the world couldn't prepare me. I was bewildered. Anything could happen. This spooked me. Panic coursed through my body the day before I was released. My sense of trepidation pulsated with an insistent beat. I looked at the clock with anxiety.

"What's wrong, dude? You're getting out tomorrow. You should be jumping for joy. Instead, you look glum," Gary said perceptively.

"Yeah. I guess I'm nervous," I replied.

"That's understandable but you'll be OK."

"I don't know, bro. I could end up right back here."

"Nah. Just be careful. Don't you have somewhere to go? I know you were in foster homes but don't you have some friends to turn to?" Gary asked.

"Nope."

"What are you going to do?"

"That's what I've been trying to figure out," I replied.

"What did you do before you got locked up?"

"I slept in a stolen car."

"Oh. That's not good."

"Nope. It isn't. I might have to do it again, though."

"Well, uh, at least you are getting out during the summertime. You can sleep during the day and stay up at night."

"Yeah, I don't know. I'm not too worried about sleeping. I barely sleep anyway."

"I know, man. Don't think I didn't notice you tossing and turning every night."

"Oh, wow. You noticed."

"Yep. Do you get nightmares or something?"

"Yes. Bad ones."

"That sucks," he said.

"For sure," I said.

"So, what is the tentative game plan?" he asked.

"I'm going to go to my probation officer's office and then

head to Greenwood," I said.

"Then what?" he asked quizzically.

"That's it," I said hopelessly.

"That's it? You've got to have more of a plan than that."

"That's as far as I've gotten," I said somberly.

"Wow. You're right to be nervous. Anything could happen."

"Yep," I said.

Tragedy revisited me on numerous occasions, including this one.

And it does.

To be continued…

Epilogue

—◇o⟨⟩o◇—

This book was nearly impossible to write. The last year of school that I completed was the sixth grade.

I did not write this to gain pity or sympathy. I needed to write it. It had to be written. People need to know about my situation. People need to know what abandonment and abuse can do to any child. It is unconscionable and unbelievably damaging to abandon children. I have decided to become the poster boy for this damage. I want the world to know what can happen. I want everyone in the world to point at me and say, "Do you see him? His life was absolutely ruined because of what happened to him during his childhood." There is no question in my mind that certain childhood events propelled me down the road of destruction. Anyone who says otherwise is out of touch. We need to bring this conversation to the forefront. We should not relegate this conversation to the shadows. All foster kids and abuse victims need to know that they are not alone. In the second book, *A Street Kid's Manifesto*, you will witness my atrocious disintegration. I do not say this lightly. It will shock you. My years of homelessness put me in the middle of the devil's playground. I was robbed three times. I was assaulted. In self-defense, I was forced to shoot at people on two different occasions. I watched my best friend get stabbed to death while I was being viciously jumped.

You will find out why I felt his blood was on my hands? I will detail my two suicide attempts, my numerous high-speed chases with the police, and my further activities as a criminal. I ultimately became rich on the streets. This inadvertently made me a target for both friends and foes. Additionally, I was incarcerated repeatedly. You will learn about how hard it was for me to enter an adult prison for the first time. I was regularly released without adequate guidance, resources, or knowledge. Consequently, I continued my wayward march into criminality. With the US Marshals on my tail, I crossed the country to confront my father in Tennessee.

I am propelled by my need to know the truth before it is too late. You will find out why my father initially put me in foster care. You will learn about my mother's downward spiral, my response to it, and her reasoning for abandoning me. I ultimately suffer a severe mental breakdown. You will learn about it all. You know the alpha, but you need to know the omega. You cannot read one without the other. You need the full picture.

In my third book, *A Convict's Manifesto*, you will be stunned and startled by the savage attack that nearly killed me. I needed multiple staples and stitches. I survived but my triumph was short-lived. A different vicious threat quickly jeopardized my life. People exploited my declining mental health and my lack of education to hastily bulldoze my case through an absurd and bizarre trial. There was no defense. There was no one to argue the merits of my case. Beguiled by the superior court judge of King County and the prosecutor, I argued nonsensically and unrealistically that I had sovereignty. I claimed that I was my own foreign state. I told them that I was immune from their jurisdiction. Unsurprisingly, the absurd trial was a mockery. My delusions had led me to make paranoid and illogical arguments. On the order of the judge, the King County sheriff forcibly took my fingerprints. The physical and mental pain was excruciating. The aftereffects of this miscarriage of justice were unbearable, crushing, and absolutely devastating. After many years, I have finally recovered my lucidity. I have found the clarity and the strength to expose this terrible injustice for everyone to see. The people can determine their own opinions about whether or not the court's judgment on me was rushed

In conclusion, I want to thank you from the bottom of my heart for your time and attention. You are an inspiration. You are my guiding force. Without your presence, my bleak existence would be unimaginable, abhorrent, and forbidding. You give me the hope and vigor to keep fighting the demons of my injustice. You help me fight to recover. I know now that it is possible for me to turn my life around. I am redeemable. I refuse to allow my abusers to win. It is an uphill battle, but with your support, guidance, and direction I will make it. I am positive of that. Thank you.

Afterwords

T he painful process of recounting this story has unchained me from my dreadful secrets. However, I have not addressed everything. I have much more to say. I need to shed these tears so that I can heal my soul. It is no secret that this arduous journey has been extremely hard on me.

As I wrote down my story, it became tougher for me to frame my message. It hurt badly. Torrent of tears soaked my manuscript. Please do not judge my story by any particular section of weak writing. Instead, please understand the intense effort that I have put into this book. You will have to bear with me throughout this entire trilogy. This is the first time I've written anything.

My dream is to speak publicly about my life with kids who are at risk. I specifically want to talk to foster kids. I want to discuss the sexual abuse and the abandonment that I experienced, but I also want to discuss peer pressure, drugs, criminality, and violence. I have so much to offer. I can help kids who are in trouble because I have been through tough times.

My dream is to go around the world and champion kids who

are in trouble. By reading this trilogy, you are participating in a humanitarian effort. For that, I thank you. You are amazing and you are more than a confidant. You are my friend. As you will see in the third book of this trilogy, I will have to overcome some obstacles before I can achieve my dream. I can conquer these problems and achieve my goal to help kids.

By exposing my sordid past, I aim to help kids who are in trouble. Thank you for bearing with me. To achieve this goal, I hope that you will consider contributing your time or your resources to the nonprofit Hopeless Kids Foundation.

THE HOPELESS CAMPAIGN

———◇○◯◯◯○◇———

This trilogy is a compelling look at America few get to see. Every American needs to learn about the tragedy of the author's life. No one should be denied this opportunity. We can all gather some important wisdom from this story. We can do a huge public service by spreading the news about it. We the people can make a difference. We cannot stand by idly and accept the abuse and injustice that the author has experienced. Take this message to everyone you know. Take it to people you don't know. Collectively, we can bring awareness to the issues of abandonment, sexual abuse, and injustice. There are many ways to do this. Here are a few:

• You can spread the word online through social media, blogging, twitter, texting, emailing, etc.

• You can create your own website dedicated to promoting this trilogy. This is a once-in-a-lifetime story that needs to be told. Who can you share it with?

• You can create video reviews to upload onto YouTube, Yelp, Tudou, or other media or web outlets. The goal is for these videos to go viral. You can even utilize satirical or unique approaches. Use your imagination.

• You can make billboards or signs to place in the windows of your car, your house, or your business. Be creative. Bring a sign to sporting games.

• You can buy multiple copies of this book wholesale and sell them personally through a brick-and-mortar business, a web business, or your place of employment. You can even go door to door with them or sell them at a church bookstore.

• You can donate books to abuse shelters, victims of sexual abuse, mental health facilities, drug and alcohol treatment facilities, prisons, jails, and homeless shelters. People at these places need to know that they are not alone.

• You can demand that local bookstores, libraries, grocery stores, coffee shops, airplane bookstores, and convenience stores stock these books. Together, we can do this. If we don't do this, who will?

• Do you know someone famous? You can tell him or her about this book. You can request that he or she spread the message. Are you following a star on twitter or any other social media outlet? You can urge them to take part in this campaign.

• You can write a review in your local newspaper, your favorite magazine, or a newsletter.

• You can go to the Good Reads website or any other forum to share how you felt about this book. Did you feel the author's pain? Was it well articulated? Share your thoughts.

• You can contact local, national, and international media outlets, such as CNN, CBS, ABC, NBC, and Fox. You can request that they interview the author and highlight and discuss the book. Together, we can compel people to take notice.

• You can talk about the book in a group environment. At church, Alcoholics Anonymous meetings, or work meetings, you can give a speech about how the author's rough life has impacted you.

• Are you in school? You can bring the message to your classmates. You can mention how the author never went to school after the sixth grade. It is inspiring that he was able to expose his story. It took immense courage for him to do so. Let's repay him by taking the initiative to spread the word.

• You can organize rallies, walks, marathons, marches, and meetings against hopelessness. We can make a statement together about how sexual abuse is unacceptable.

• At Christmas time, you can give a copy of this book to friends, family members, or co-workers. Let's share the message about how lucky we are to have family members who love us. Remember when the author looked into that window on Christmas? You can share this compelling story.

• Do you have resources to donate to advertisements, commercials, or billboards? This is a good cause to get involved in. Go to the website and donate.

• You can become a regional representative. For more information, go to www.hopelessinseattlebook.com.

• Do you have any other ideas to spread the message? We need volunteers to transcribe the trilogy into different languages.

• To become more engaged, go to www.hopelessinseattlebook. com, where you can print brochures, banners, car advertisements, etc. You can interact with the host of the website, other fans, and support members. You can leave testimonials. As the Pledge of Allegiance says, "Together we stand; divided we fall." This movement will fall unless people like you stand up and take initiative. You are strong, important, and persuasive. Your voice does matter. We need you. Foster kids need you. Abuse victims need you. The author needs you. Commit to making a difference.

THE HOPELESS KIDS FOUNDATION

⬥⟶∘⟨⟩∘⟵⬥

This grassroots nonprofit organization plans to work for forgotten, hopeless children. It is committed to making a difference in their lives. The hopeless ones are the most vulnerable kids and adults that society has neglected. The hopeless are completely undefended, unprotected, and unguarded. Hopeless people are current and former foster kids, homeless kids, juvenile delinquents, victims of sexual and child abuse, people with poor mental health, criminals, and drug addicts. This foundation aims to help all hopeless people. However, the foundation is in its infancy. It is not funded by any government agencies. The readers are the sole underwriters. Donations are desperately needed. We need used clothing, electronics, shoes, and cars that are in good condition. All donations are tax-deductible. Every dollar counts. You can set jars on the countertops of your businesses, churches, and schools. Collectively, we can fund this foundation.

You can also show your support by buying trendy clothes and accessories from the Hopeless Kids Foundation. These items will make a loud and clear statement that you are supporting forgotten and hopeless kids in many different ways. For instance, they desperately need counseling. Most hopeless kids have no one to talk to. They have no parents and no family members. They have nothing. We seek to change that. We also hope to enlist the help of mentors and spiritual advisers. We need people to individually guide and shepherd these hopeless kids. If you would like to volunteer, please do so on the website. We need to help hopeless people reintegrate into society. Like the author, most of them have no one to turn to. We plan to give them resources that they can depend on when they are released from juvenile or adult detention facilities. We will help them get temporary or long-term shelter. We will help them find work. Do you have a room, a basement, a guesthouse, some rental property, or a mobile home that you would consider offering to help a hopeless person? Can you offer employment? If you can help out, please notify the webmaster.

Society grossly disregards and ignores hopeless people. Tough-on-crime initiatives have preyed on them. This perpetual and vicious cycle needs to be stopped. Imagine your son, daughter, brother, or sister being lost in the foster care system. Would you want an organization like the Hopeless Kids Foundation to be there? Even if their thoughts, emotions, and actions caused them to be incarcerated, they need help. If you want to be a part of the solution by providing the safety net that currently is not there, then please log onto www.hopelessinseattlebook.com to donate, volunteer, or purchase gear and clothing. Remember, this is a movement. One penny at a time, we can change the lives of hopeless people. Thank you for being you.

Biography

Daniel Simms was born on October 2, 1980, at Northwest Hospital in Seattle. He is a born-again Christian who found his faith in a dark place. He has hopes and dreams that he is trying to achieve while he is incarcerated. In addition to his GED, he has also achieved his paralegal certificate. In his spare time, he likes to stay up to date with current events by reading as much as he can. He has a thirst for knowledge. He has one son, Dillon.

Dedication

I would like to dedicate this book to all the people engaged in reversing the trend of America's reliance on Mass Incarceration. Understanding the true cost on families, society, and individuals is the first step. Ninety-percent of inmates suffer from Mental Health and Addiction. That is their true malady. Let us find a more sane approach. If society provided treatment instead of incarceration it would destroy this insane recidivism rate.

Some seventy percent of inmates return to prison in the first three years upon release. That is not solely due to the inmate. Society needs to bear some of that blame. And I am extremely thankful dialogue has begun on this dire topic.